Key History
for

South Africa

Hamish Macdonald and
Barry Williamson

Stanley Thornes (Publishers) Ltd

Original design by Hilary Norman
Typesetting and layout by Raynor Design
Illustrations by Hardlines, Linda Lancaster (p. 22), Mick Stubbs
(p. 27) and John York (p. 34)
Picture research by Julia Hanson

Original line illustrations © Stanley Thornes (Publishers) Ltd
1997

First published in 1997 by:
Stanley Thornes (Publishers) Ltd
Ellenborough House
Wellington Street
CHELTENHAM GL50 1YW
England

97 98 99 00 / 10 9 8 7 6 5 4 3 2 1

A catalogue record for this book is available from the British
Library.

ISBN 0–7487–2585–7

Cover photograph: Rex Features

Printed in Hong Kong by Dah Hua Printing Co. Ltd.

Acknowledgements

The authors and publishers are grateful to the following for
permission to reproduce illustrations and photographs:

Albany Museum: 15 left;
Archive Photos, New York: 70 bottom;
Art Publishers, South Africa: 7 bottom, 16 top left, 31 both;
AP/Sasa Kralj: 92 right;
Bailey's African History Archives: 25 bottom right, 37
    right, (Gopal Naransamy) 54 left;
Bodleian Library/E. Lee Collection: 18;
The British Library, London: 21 right (MC 1587);
Camera Press: 32, 44 top, 68, 72;
Killie Campbell Africana Library, University of Natal: 28
    both, 29;
Cape Archives Depot: 15 right (AG 15775);
Courtesy of The Cape Times: 42;
Corbis-Bettmann: (Reuters) 84 top & bottom, 86, 87 right,
    89 top & bottom, 90 bottom, 91, (UPI) 58 bottom;
ET Archive: 16 bottom right;
William Fehr Collection, Cape Town: 12;
Courtesy of Gallo Music Publishers: 64;
The Hutchison Library: 10 right;
IDAF Collection, Mayibuye Centre: 4, 5 right, 21 left, 23,
    24, 25 left & top right, 35, 37 left, 38 left, 38–9, 41, 44
    bottom, 45 bottom, 49, 55, 56, 66 top, 67 top, 80;
Reproduced by permission of the Estate of Helen Joseph: 50;
Courtesy of Mrs. Enid Kenyon: 63 bottom;
Museum Africa: 13, 20, 30;
National Portrait Gallery, London: 58 top;
Network/Gideon Mendel: 94;
Peter Newark's Pictures: 17;
Oliphant copyright Universal Press Syndicate. Reprinted
    with permission. All rights reserved: 45 top;
Pix Features: 74;
Popperfoto: 33 top, 40, 47, 71, 81, 87 bottom left,
    (Reuters) 93,
(David Thomson/Reuters) 95;
The Rand Daily Mail (Courtesy Times Media Limited,
    Johannesburg): 33 bottom;
Rex Features: 5 left, 8, 10 left, 69, 76, 77, 79, 82;
Courtesy South Africa Tourism Board: 7 top;
South African Library: 52, 57;
The Star, Johannesburg: 51;
War Museum of the Boer Republics, Bloemfontein: 19 both.

Every effort has been made to contact copyright holders
and we apologise if any have been inadvertently
overlooked.

We are particularly grateful for help and advice from: Jo
Emery, Rose Gaynor, Rob Sieborger, Gail and Tich Walker,
Robert Morrell and George Warman.

Contents

1 'This beautiful country . . .'

1964–94: 'An ideal for which I am prepared to die . . .'

 What was apartheid?

White people are a minority in South Africa (Source **A**).

Source A   South Africa's main ethnic groups

	Million people	%
Black	31.5	76
White	5.4	13
Asian (mainly Indian)	1.2	3
Coloured	3.3	8
Total	41.4	100

South Africa: After Apartheid – Understanding Global Issues, **1995**

Nevertheless, between 1652 and 1900 they took over South Africa and refused to share power with non-whites. Instead, during the twentieth century they created a system of laws to prevent non-whites from gaining political or economic power.

This system became known as *apartheid* – pronounced 'apart-hate', meaning to be apart or separate (Source **B**).

Source B   The system of apartheid

- Members of the Government had to be white.
- Many jobs were for whites only.
- Only 13% of the land of South Africa was allocated to blacks.
- In towns whites and blacks had to live in separate areas.
- Marriage or sex between people from different racial groups was banned.
- All South Africans had to register as either Black, White, Asian or Coloured and carry passes to control where they could and could not go.
- Whites and non-whites had to use separate public toilets, swimming baths, park benches, shops, beaches, cinemas, buses, ambulances, hospitals and other amenities.
- Severe penalties for disobeying or protesting against apartheid included fines, beatings and prison.

In 1964 Nelson Mandela and others were sentenced to life imprisonment for trying to overthrow apartheid (Source **C**).

Source C   Nelson Mandela and Walter Sisulu in prison on Robben Island in 1966

Source D Nelson Mandela at his trial in April 1964

During my lifetime I have dedicated myself to the struggle of the African people. I have fought against white domination, and I have fought against black domination. I have cherished the ideal of a democratic and free society in which all persons live together in harmony and with equal opportunities. It is an ideal which I hope to live for and to achieve. But if needs be it is an ideal for which I am prepared to die.

Mandela repeated these words 27 years later immediately after the white government set him free. Four years later on 10 May 1994 he became President of South Africa (Source **E**).

Source E Nelson Mandela becomes President of South Africa

Apartheid had become history but millions of non-white South Africans had paid a cruel price for their freedom (Source **F**).

Source F Hector Peterson, aged 13, the first to be shot by police during protests by school children in Soweto, 16 June 1976

1 Use Source **A** to make a pie chart.
   a) Convert the percentage figures into degrees by multiplying each by 3.6. The new figures should add up to a total of 360.
   b) Use a protractor to measure and draw the angles. Use a different colour for each segment.

2 Choose a partner.
   a) Make notes for a speech describing your feelings about apartheid using Source **B**. Take it in turns to practise your speech.

 *Questions*

   b) Together read Source **D**. On your own write down an 'ideal' for which you would be prepared to die or spend your life in prison, then discuss it with your partner.

3 Compare Sources **C** and **E**.
   a) What looks different about Nelson Mandela and why?
   b) Use Source **D** to explain what had not changed.
   c) How do Sources **A**, **B** and **F** help explain why Mandela was still prepared to pay a heavy price for his ideal, even after 27 years in prison?

Views of South Africa

What does South Africa look like?

F. W. de Klerk became President of South Africa in 1989 at a time when his worst fears seemed to be coming true.

Source A F. W. de Klerk, Cape Town, December 1983

This beautiful country, this land of milk and honey, this country bought so dearly – if we do not act correctly and in time – can be changed into a country of blood and hatred, revolution and crisis.

In 1990, it was F. W. de Klerk who decided to release Nelson Mandela from prison and helped to bring an end to apartheid.

Source B Nelson Mandela, in his first speech after having replaced de Klerk as President in 1994

Never, never, and never again shall it be that this beautiful land will experience the oppression of one by another and suffer the indignity of being the skunk of the world.

South Africa is five times the size of the United Kingdom. From the southern tip of the continent of Africa the furthest it stretches north is 2000 km. At its widest from west to east, South Africa is 1500 km (Source **C**).

Source C Physical map of Southern Africa

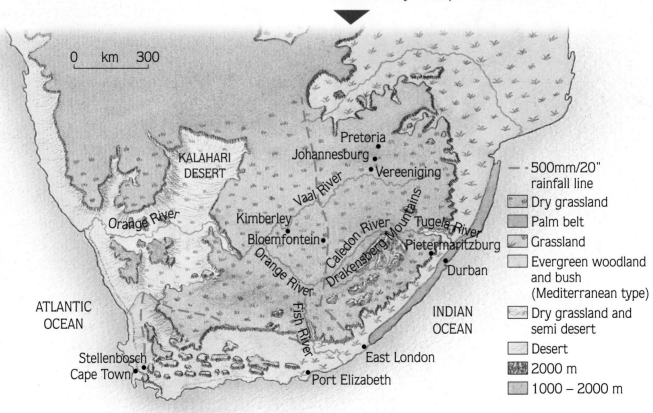

South Africa a world in one country

It is a country of spectacular scenery ranging from the sand dunes of the Kalahari desert in the Northwest to the great semi-dry plateau of the high grassland (veld), from the Drakensberg mountains, coastal forests, lowland meadows and sub-tropical surf beaches, to the mountains and vineyards which surround the Southern Cape (Source **D**).

South Africa is rich in wildlife, minerals and farmland. Swallowed up in this vast landscape there are also some ugly sights: skyscraper cities like Johannesburg, with sprawling and squalid townships like Soweto, spoil tips from mines, busy industrial centres with factories and smelting plants, power stations, oil refineries and the grimy dockland areas of the big ports.

Source D   South African Tourist Board calendar, 1995

Source E   Aerial photograph of the Southern Cape

Questions

1   Why do you think F. W. de Klerk had reason to refer to 'blood, hatred, revolution and crisis' in South Africa in 1983 (Source **A**)?

2   Read Source **B**. How does Mandela sum up world opinion of South Africa before the end of apartheid?

3   Look at Sources **C** and **D**.
   a) What scenes of South Africa does Source **D** not show?

b) Can you suggest why these scenes are not shown in this source?

c) Imagine a journey by air from the Kalahari desert to Durban. Describe the changes of scenery below.

4   Both de Klerk and Mandela describe South Africa as a 'beautiful country'. After looking at Sources **C**, **D** and **E** do you think they are telling the truth or just being patriotic?

The peoples of South Africa

 ## Who are the South Africans?

The languages and cultures of South Africa

The South Africans are a mixture of many peoples who share a country where there has been a history of extreme racism. To those in power during the time of apartheid, racial differences were important. They classified themselves as 'whites' and those who were not as 'Blacks, Asians and Coloureds (those of mixed race)'. Those who were not 'white' were the victims of the racist system of apartheid. Black South Africans, who are the majority, belong to different nations and tribal groups which have different languages and cultures. There are also language and cultural differences between South African whites and South African Asians.

Source A A street in the city of Johannesburg in South Africa

During the time of apartheid there were just two official languages: Afrikaans and English – both languages of the whites. Today, eleven official languages are spoken in South Africa (Source **B**).

Source B Official languages and migrations in South Africa

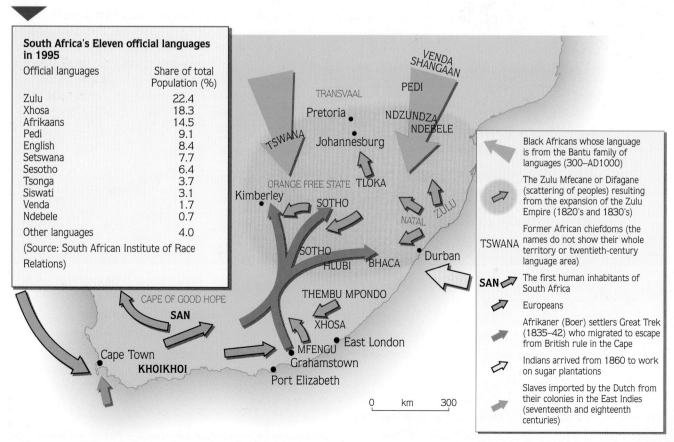

South Africa's Eleven official languages in 1995	
Official languages	Share of total Population (%)
Zulu	22.4
Xhosa	18.3
Afrikaans	14.5
Pedi	9.1
English	8.4
Setswana	7.7
Sesotho	6.4
Tsonga	3.7
Siswati	3.1
Venda	1.7
Ndebele	0.7
Other languages	4.0
(Source: South African Institute of Race Relations)	

Black Africans whose language is from the Bantu family of languages (300–AD1000)

The Zulu Mfecane or Difagane (scattering of peoples) resulting from the expansion of the Zulu Empire (1820's and 1830's)

Former African chiefdoms (the names do not show their whole territory or twentieth-century language area)

The first human inhabitants of South Africa

Europeans

Afrikaner (Boer) settlers Great Trek (1835–42) who migrated to escape from British rule in the Cape

Indians arrived from 1860 to work on sugar plantations

Slaves imported by the Dutch from their colonies in the East Indies (seventeenth and eighteenth centuries)

Who were the first South Africans?

There are no written records for the early history of South Africa. What we know comes from a few physical remains and the oral tradition of story-telling. The evidence of cave paintings suggests that the first inhabitants of South Africa were the San or Bushmen. They did not build permanent homes but depended on hunting and moving in search of food. Some San still live in this way in parts of the Kalahari desert and Namibia. Next to arrive, about 3000 years ago, were cattle farmers – the Khoikhoi tribes. Their language, like the San, uses click sounds which may be how they got the Afrikaner nickname, 'Hottentots'.

The migration of the Nguni

Both San and Khoikhoi are yellow-skinned. It is thought that black Africans migrated from the north between 300 and 1000 AD. Among them were the Nguni who settled in the South Eastern region of South Africa.

Source C By Nelson Mandela

The Nguni can be divided into a northern group – the Zulu and the Swazi people – and a Southern group, ... the Xhosa nation. ... Each Xhosa belongs to a clan that traces its descent back to a specific forefather. I am a member of the Madiba clan, named after a Thembu chief who ruled in the Transkei in the eighteenth century. I am often addressed as Madiba, my clan name, as a sign of respect.

From *Long Walk to Freedom*, 1994

The Nguni brought with them knowledge of crop farming and iron making. By the time Europeans and Asians began to arrive, in the fifteenth century, South Africa already had a complicated society of many languages and cultures.

Europeans and Asians arrive

The safe harbour of the Cape of Good Hope first attracted Europeans who were looking for a new trade route to India and the Far East. It was a good place to rest and refuel with supplies of fresh water, fruit and vegetables. In 1652 the Dutch East India company set up a permanent settlement at Table Bay. Here the Dutch imported slaves from Mozambique, Madagascar, India, Ceylon and Malaysia, and brought political prisoners – some of whom they imprisoned on Robben Island. Germans and French Huguenots also settled near the Cape. Later the British, who were at war with France, took over the Cape from the Dutch, first temporarily in 1795 and then permanently in 1805 in order to protect their trade route to India.

The Mfecane

During the early part of the nineteenth century violent changes and migrations took place among the Nguni, known as the Mfecane (Source **B**). From these changes emerged a large Zulu empire and the resettlement of the other African tribes and nations which Europeans found as they moved inland.

The Europeans who migrated inland were Dutch-speaking Afrikaners or Boers who wanted to escape from British rule in the Cape. However, even after they set up self-governing territories, known as the Orange Free State and the Transvaal, the British would not leave them alone. One of the main reasons was the discovery there of rich deposits of diamonds in 1867 and gold in 1871.

From the 1860s European farmers imported Indian labourers to work on their sugar plantations in the coastal province of Natal – work which the proud Zulus were unwilling to do. Soon Indian merchants began to see opportunities to set up businesses in South Africa.

Later immigrants and settlers included Jewish refugees from the Baltic after the First World War, and more Dutch and Germans after the Second World War. In the 1960s Greek immigrants arrived from Cyprus and Portuguese came from Madeira and former Portuguese colonies. Immigrants from Eastern Europe also arrived after the Soviet invasions of Hungary (1956) and Czechoslovakia (1968).

Questions

1 What do Sources **A**, **B** and **C** tell you about who the different peoples of South Africa are?

2 **a)** Make a timeline to show the different migrations both to and inside South Africa.
   b) What were the different causes of these migrations?

3 **a)** Why do you think the history of migration has made it difficult to unite the peoples of South Africa?
   b) Suggest which peoples' migrations may have caused most conflict and why?

A land of contrasts

▶ *What problems remained after the end of apartheid?*

Rich versus poor

The end of apartheid and white minority rule did not bring an end to South Africa's problems. An immediately obvious contrast in South Africa is between wealth and poverty (Sources **A** and **B**).

Source A   Aerial photograph of a northern suburb of Johannesburg

Source B   Photograph of homes in Soweto

In 1995, of the 41.4 million people living in South Africa, 13% owned 75% of the land. A mere 5% of the population – mostly white people – owned 88% of South Africa's wealth. On average, the homes of white families had more than eight times more floor space than the homes of black families. The homes of over 20 million people in 1993 had no electricity or adequate sanitation.

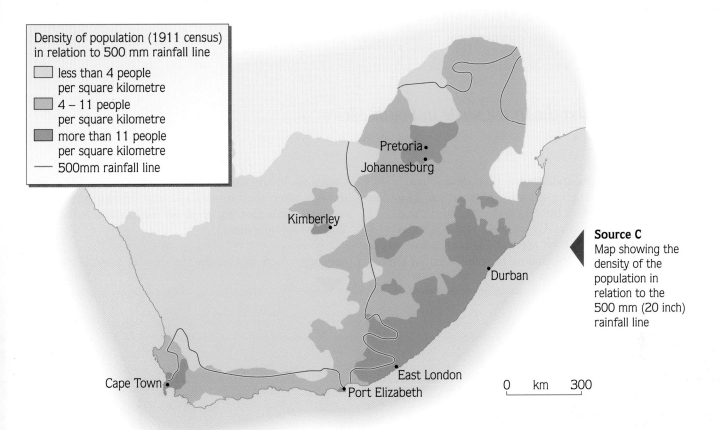

Density of population (1911 census) in relation to 500 mm rainfall line

- [ ] less than 4 people per square kilometre
- [ ] 4 – 11 people per square kilometre
- [ ] more than 11 people per square kilometre
- — 500mm rainfall line

Pretoria•
Johannesburg•

Kimberley•

Durban•

East London
Port Elizabeth

Cape Town•

0   km   300

Source C
Map showing the density of the population in relation to the 500 mm (20 inch) rainfall line

Town versus country

Another contrast is between the countryside (rural areas) and towns and cities (urban areas) of South Africa. Only 13% of South Africa is suitable for crop farming. Nearly all this farmland in 1995 was owned by whites. During the twentieth century the proportion of the population living in urban areas increased dramatically (Source **D**).

Source D   The percentage of the population living in towns

	All	White	Coloured	Asian	African
1904	23	53	49	36	10
1951	43	78	65	78	27
1991	63	91	83	96	58

From William Beinart, *Twentieth Century South Africa*, OUP, 1994

The causes of conflict

Apartheid and white minority rule left behind them an unequal distribution of wealth, land and jobs – a country in which the white minority continued to get richer while almost half the population earned scarcely enough to live on. How easy would it be to build a nation without conflict when six million adults could not read or write, 40% dropped out of school by the age of 10, 50% of young black South Africans were unemployed and only 5% of senior management positions in industry were held by blacks?

Questions

1 Look at Sources **A** and **B**.
   a) Suggest which of these photographs shows the homes of white people and which shows the homes of black people. Explain your answer.
   b) Identify and describe the clues which show the differences between wealth and poverty.

2 Look at the rainfall line in Source **C**.
   a) Why do you think more people chose to settle on land to the east of this line?
   b) Who owned most of this land in 1995?

3 Study Source **D**.
   a) What change does this show in where people lived between 1904 and 1991?
   b) Use the information on pages 10 and 11 to suggest whether this change would have made relations between whites and blacks better or worse. Give reasons for your answer.

11

2 The roots of conflict

The invasion of the whites

 Why did the Dutch settle in South Africa?

In 1952, Africans, Indians and Coloureds joined together to defy the unjust laws of apartheid. They had a special reason for choosing 6 April to begin their defiance. This was the day in 1652 when Jan van Riebeeck arrived in the Cape to build a refreshment station to supply ships trading for the Dutch East India Company. While Afrikaners annually celebrate this as the day when their ancestors arrived, black Africans see it as the beginning of an invasion which led to slavery and apartheid.

Source A   Table Bay showing the arrival of a fleet of ships

The Dutch East India company

At first the Dutch East India company just wanted to farm a small area of land to grow crops and to obtain supplies of meat by trading with the Khoikhoi. The Khoikhoi showed some resistance to the taking of land, but took advantage of the opportunity to trade cattle for iron and copper. To keep the cost of labour as low as possible and to avoid trouble with the Khoikhoi, the Dutch brought slaves from other parts of Africa and the East Indies to work for them. Then, to save more money, the Dutch East India Company released some soldiers from their service to become independent farmers.

Source B   Trekboers, by Samuel Daniel

The settlers move inland

Most of these soldiers were Dutch but among them were Germans, Scandinavians, French and a few English. Later, refugees from France, known as Huguenots, joined them. These settlers soon found they had three things in common:
- a Protestant form of Christianity
- a simple way of life based on farming
- a new language called Afrikaans – a version of Dutch which mixed in new words from speaking to each other and to their slaves and servants.

They proudly accepted the name, 'Boers', which means 'farmers'. The Boers began to resent the authority of the Dutch East India Company who ruled at the Cape. Horses imported to the Cape in the 1660s made it easier for some Boers to become wandering cattle farmers known as 'trekboers' (Source **B**) and to explore further inland.

In 1705 a Company trader hoping to trade for oxen with the Khoikhoi found that a trekboer had got there before him (Source **C**).

Mounted and armed with superior weapons, whites easily smashed the resistance of the Khoikhoi and the remaining San. Many of those who survived became their servants. The 'coloureds' in the Cape descend from the children of mixed marriages between the Khoikhoi, the yellow-skinned San, slaves and some of their white masters.

Source C   Johannes Starrenburg, the magistrate of Stellenbosch, writing about his travels in 1705

[T]he trekboer had] chased out the Hottentots, set fire to their huts, and took away all their cattle, without their knowing for what reason since they had never harmed any of the Dutch. By this they lost everything they had.

Questions

1 **a)** What do Afrikaners celebrate on 6 April (Source **A**)?
   b) Why was this day chosen in 1952 as the day to begin a defiance campaign against apartheid?

2 Explain the terms 'Boers', 'trekboers' and 'Coloureds'.

3 What clues do Sources **B** and **C** give about the trekboers way of life?

The British conquest

 What were the consequences of the British settlement in South Africa?

Trade

Protection of the trade route to India was Britain's motive for taking over the Cape, first in 1795 and again in 1806. Then, between 1820 and 1824, Britain encouraged large numbers of British settlers to emigrate to South Africa to ease the problem of unemployment in Britain and to help defend the Cape Colony's eastern frontier.

Frontier wars

The British settlers built new towns at Port Elizabeth and Grahamstown (Source **A**). Droughts and overpopulation led to growing tension between the Europeans and the Xhosa, who fiercely resisted when Boer farmers and the new settlers took more Xhosa land. It took the British eight frontier wars, between 1819 and 1853, to defeat the Xhosa finally. Source **B** shows the British cavalry charge at the Battle of Gwangqua in 1846 in which 500 Xhosa died.

The Great Trek and independent Boer states

The British took over the Cape in 1806, and abolished the slave trade in 1807 and slavery in 1833. The Boers found this and other attempts to impose British laws on them unbearable. Between 1834 and 1840 15,000 Boers tried to escape from the British by leaving their farms and migrating inland. They came to be known as 'Voortrekkers'. Powerful resistance from the Xhosa in the east forced the Voortrekkers north, across the Orange and Vaal rivers, and then eastwards across the Drakensberg mountains into Natal. Today, their descendants, the Afrikaners, remember this epic journey as 'the Great Trek'

After a famous victory against the Zulus at Blood river in 1838 the Boers tried to set up an independent republic in Natal. However, the British would not leave them alone. Britain took over Natal in 1843 and ruled it as another colony in addition to the Cape. The British allowed the Zulus their own land to the north of the Tugela and east of Buffalo rivers. The Boers, however, did not give up. Despite African resistance and British opposition, they succeeded in forming independent

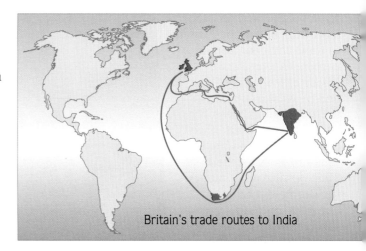

Britain's trade routes to India

states in the Transvaal (the South African Republic, 1852) and the Orange Free State (1854). In the Transvaal the Boers made new slaves by kidnapping African children whom they called 'inboekselings'.

Indian South Africans

Sugar produced from cane grown in Natal from 1851 provided a new source of wealth, but there was a shortage of labour. Unable to persuade Africans to work for them the sugar plantation owners recruited labourers from India (Source **C**). Between 1860 and 1911, with government help, they paid for 152,000 Indians to come to Natal. About 52% decided to stay in southern Africa when their contracts ended.

Question

1 What different motives did the British have for setting up colonies in South Africa shown in Source **A** before 1870?

2 Describe the consequences of British settlement in South Africa shown in Sources **A**, **B** and **C** for **a)** the Boers, **b)** Black Africans, and **c)** the population of Natal today.

3 What do Sources **B** and **C** tell us about the different methods the British used to take control of the Cape and Natal?

Source A British and Boer advances into the interior by 1870

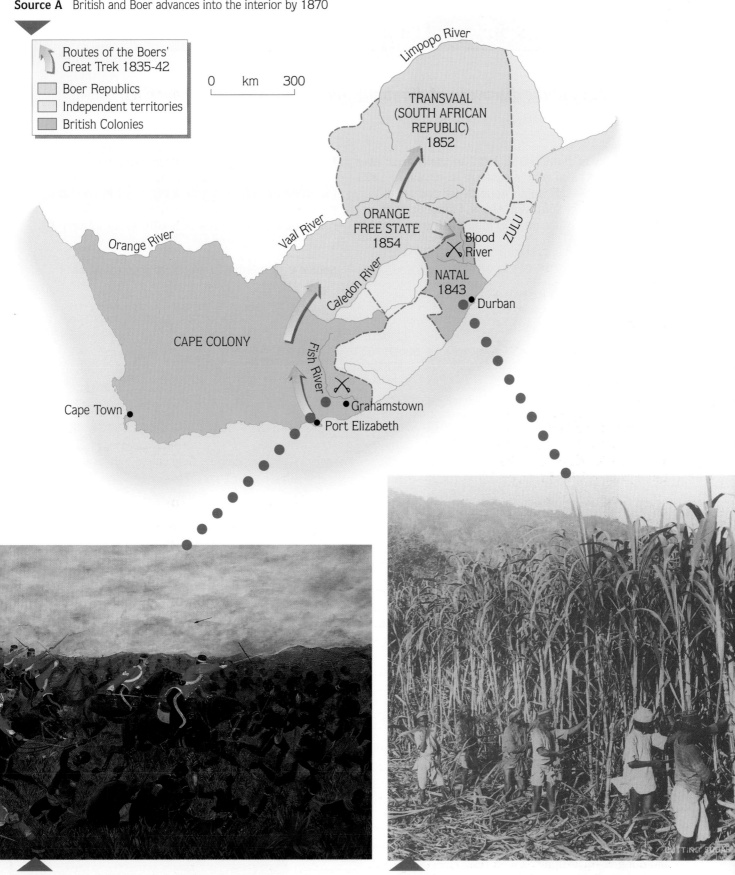

Legend:
- Routes of the Boers' Great Trek 1835-42
- Boer Republics
- Independent territories
- British Colonies

0 km 300

Limpopo River

TRANSVAAL (SOUTH AFRICAN REPUBLIC) 1852

ORANGE FREE STATE 1854

Orange River

Vaal River

Caledon River

ZULU

Blood River

NATAL 1843

Durban

CAPE COLONY

Fish River

Grahamstown

Port Elizabeth

Cape Town

Source B The Battle of Gwangqua, 1846

Source C Indians working on a sugar plantation in Natal

15

Diamonds, gold and empire!

▶ Why did the discovery of diamonds and gold increase the conflict?

The discovery of diamonds in 1867 in the Orange river area (Source **A**) and gold in eastern Transvaal in 1871 suddenly increased Britain's appetite for control of more territories in Southern Africa. Competition from Britain's rivals, France and Germany, led to a scramble to add parts of Africa to their growing empires. Pressure from ambitious businessmen in the Cape like the mine owner, Cecil Rhodes (Source **B**), and from white settlers in Natal spurred the British on to complete their conquest of South Africa (Source **C**).

Source A   The Big Hole at Kimberley (mining for diamonds stopped here in 1914)

Source C   The British 'scramble' for Southern Africa

GERMAN SOUTH-WEST AFRICA 1884

BECHUANALAND 1885-96

Bulawayo
RHODESIA 1890-96

PORTUGUESE EAST AFRICA

TRANSVAAL (SOUTH AFRICAN REPUBLIC)

Witwatersrand
Gold 1886
Johannesburg

Lourenço Marques

BRITISH BECHUANALAND 1885-95

ORANGE FREE STATE

ZULULAND 1879-97

Diamonds 1867

Kimberley   BASUTO LAND 1871

Boer republics

British territories

The direction of British expansion

0   km   300

Source B   The Rhodes Colossus

Source D   The Battle of Isandhlwana in 1879 by Charles Fripp. The Zulus won this battle but later the British defeated them and imprisoned their king, Cetshwayo

Source E A Boer 'roving field artillery' attacking the British at Mafeking

Zulu and Boer resistance

But first the British had to overcome fierce and stubborn resistance from the Zulus and the Boers. Source **D** shows a memorable victory of the Zulus over the British at the Battle of Isandhlwana before their eventual defeat. It took the British two wars to defeat the Boers in 1881 and between 1899 and 1902. In the last of these wars, Boer soldiers used their knowledge of the countryside to hide from the British and make surprise hit-and-run attacks (Source **E**) with startling success. Britain poured in 450,000 troops from all parts of its Empire to fight this much smaller army of farmers. Some 7792 British Empire soldiers died fighting and another 1300 died from illness, compared with 4000 Boer soldiers killed and 27,927 Boer women and children who died in British concentration camps. In the end Britain won what seemed a small victory which cost the British tax payer £200 million: the Boers accepted defeat with a promise of future self-government.

The Boer War of 1899–1902 proved to be a very important turning point: it shattered Britain's image of itself as a superior civilisation and military power and it brought the Boers together as a nation – a nation of 'Afrikaners'. They saw themselves as a 'white tribe' chosen by 'God', who were determined that they alone would rule South Africa – not the British and not the black Africans, Indians or Coloureds.

Questions

1 Study Sources **A**, **B** and **C**.
   a) What clue does the Big Hole at the town of Kimberley give about Britain's motives for further conquest in Southern Africa (Source **A**)?
   b) What do Sources **B** and **C** suggest about the ambition and influence of men like Cecil Rhodes?

2 Look at Source **D**. What images of the British and the Zulus do you think Charles Fripp intended when he painted this picture?

3 What does Source **E** suggest about the fighting methods of the Boers?

4 Describe British conquest of South Africa from the point of view of **a)** the Zulus, and **b)** the Boers.

5 Use the information in this chapter to design a poster which argues either for or against the view that: 'the roots of conflict in South Africa date from the beginning of British conquest.'

3 The rise of Afrikaner and African nationalism

Conflict between the Boers and the British

 What was the legacy of the Boer War for the Afrikaners?

The Boers surrendered in May 1902 and signed the Treaty of Vereeniging, but they harboured great bitterness and hatred towards the British. Much of the later history of South Africa can be explained by the working out of that hatred. It contributed to the intense feeling of national pride and independence experienced by many Afrikaners.

Source A The widow of one of the Boer soldiers, speaking in the 1970s

This war, this Boer War was the stupidest war the English ever carried on because all that they achieved was to consolidate the Afrikaner nation from the bottom of the Cape right up to Transvaal.

Quoted in David Harrison, *The White Tribe of Africa*, 1985

The Boers had two main grievances – the concentration camps and the way the English language was forced on them after the war.

The camps

By September 1900 the British assumed the war was over, but the Boers decided to continue with a guerilla war. They wrecked trains and launched commando raids. The British response was to clear the land and burn the farms which sheltered the guerillas.

Source B A British soldier

The men belonging to the farm are always away and only the women left . . . These folk we invite out into the veldt (open fields) . . . where they huddle together in their cotton frocks and big sun bonnets while our men set fire to the house . . . The women in a little group cling together comforting each other or holding their faces in each other's laps.

L. M. Phillipps, *With Rimington*, 1902

For the first time in history, many soldiers took pocket cameras with them to the battle fields. They recorded the destruction (Source **C**).

Source C Burning a Boer farm

It was then decided that the women and children from the farms should be placed in concentration camps for their comfort and safety. By November 1901 there were 113,506 people in 45 camps. The diet was poor. There was overcrowding. People who had been used to living on the open veldt had no resistance to disease caused by overcrowding and poor sanitation. There were outbreaks of scarlet fever, measles, typhoid and TB. By the end of the war the official archivist gave a total of 27,927 dead, one quarter of the total Afrikaner population in the Transvaal and Orange Free State.

A vicar's daughter from Cornwall, Emily Hobhouse, visited South Africa and returned with appalling stories of the suffering in the camps. She later translated the diary of one of the prisoners.

Source D The diary of a concentration camp prisoner, translated by Emily Hobhouse

I went one day to the hospital and there lay a child of nine years [left] to wrestle alone with death. I asked where I could find the child's mother. The answer was that the mother died a week before. . . . that morning her sister of 11 died. I pitied the poor little sufferer . . .

Emily Hobhouse, *Tant' Alie of Transvaal: Her Diary 1880–1902*

The British authorities banned Emily from making a second visit to the camps. When she died she was buried next to the Boer war heroes in Bloemfontein, the greatest honour the Afrikaners could give a foreigner.

Photographs of dead and dying children created an everlasting memory (Source **E**).

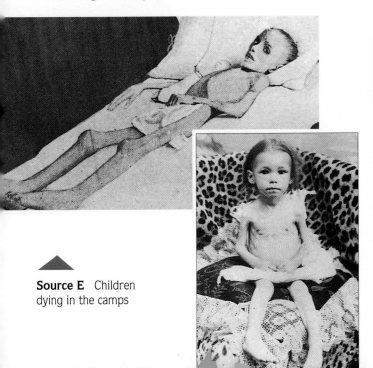

Source E Children dying in the camps

The English language

After the war, Lord Milner, the British High Commissioner, decided to promote the English language as the best way of making the Boers loyal citizens of the British Empire. English became the language of lessons in all Afrikaner schools and new English teachers were recruited from England.

Source F J. D. Vorster, a pupil at an Afrikaner school

If you were caught speaking Afrikaans you had to carry a placard round your neck bearing the words, 'I must not speak Dutch'. When the bell went for school to start again the last boy with what was called the Dutch mark had to write one thousand times, 'I must speak English at school'.

Quoted in David Harrison, *The White Tribe of Africa*, 1985

Source G Judge Marais describes the result of this new policy

Had it not been for Milner and his extreme measures, we Afrikaners would probably all quite happily have been speaking English by now. By his opposition to our language he helped create it.

Quoted in David Harrison, *The White Tribe of Africa*, 1985

The seeds sown during the war would produce a bitter harvest of Afrikaner nationalism.

Questions

1 Look at Sources **B**, **C**, **D** and **E**.
   a) What do they tell you about the methods used by the British to fight the Boers?
   b) How do these methods help explain Mrs Domisse's view that 'this Boer War was the stupidest war the English ever carried on' (Source **A**)?

2 Look at Source **F**. Write down how you would feel if you were treated in this way. Compare your answer with another student.

3 What does Judge Marais mean by saying that Milner helped to create the Afrikaans language (Source **G**)?

4 Do you think it is usually easier to fight a war than to make a peace that lasts? Give your reasons.

The legacy of the Boer War for 'the non-whites'

What had the Boer War changed?

As many as 100,000 African, Indian and Coloured people took part in the Boer War. Most of them served as labourers but Lord Kitchener armed 10,000 to help defeat the Boers. The number who died is not known. Britain claimed to be fighting to free the Africans from Boer slavery. The British government said that they wanted to extend the vote to all non-whites under the same rules as operated in the Cape. Any man there owning property worth £25 or earning more than £75 a year could automatically vote. Lord Milner, British High Commissioner in South Africa, knew this would be unacceptable to the Afrikaners. At the Peace of Vereeniging in May 1902 he included a promise that pleased the Afrikaners in Clause 8. It said that the vote would be granted to non-whites only after the Afrikaners became self-governing; in other words, never. Joseph Chamberlain, British Colonial Secretary was worried.

Source A Joseph Chamberlain's memo to Lord Milner, March 1901

We cannot consent to purchase a shameful peace by leaving the coloured population in the position in which they stood before the war, with not even the ordinary civil rights which the government of the Cape Colony has long granted them.

From the *Milner Papers*, Bodleian Library, Oxford

Why then did Britain let down the non-white people who had supported them in the war, in order to make friends with the Afrikaners they defeated? The answer is that Lord Milner believed the only way to secure South Africa's vast wealth for Britain was to make friends with the Afrikaners. Milner later said that it was the worst mistake he ever made.

The Bambatha rebellion

In Natal, in February 1906, Africans shot dead two white tax collectors. They were tracked down and killed but the protest continued. Chief Bambatha led a rebel army in the Nkandler forest. At the end of the

fighting there were almost 4000 Africans dead, including Bambatha. Only 25 white soldiers lost their lives. Bambatha's head was put on display (Source **B**).

Source B Bambatha's head

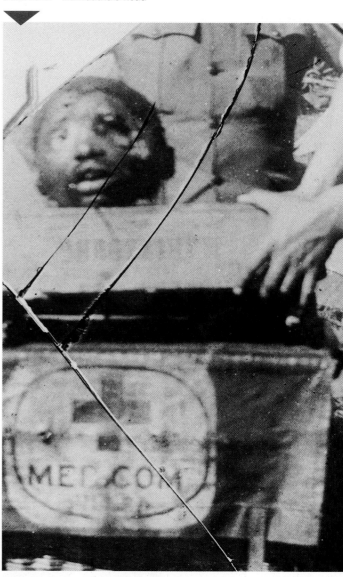

But there was no unity among the non-whites. During the Bambatha rebellion an Indian leader, M. K. Gandhi (Source **C**), organised an ambulance corps to help the government. He said he felt 'a genuine sense of loyalty to the Empire'.

Source C M. K. Gandhi

The Indians

Gandhi was an Indian lawyer who arrived in Durban in 1893. One day he was travelling by train to Pretoria. A white passenger complained about his presence in the First Class compartment. He was ejected from the train because he refused to move to a Third Class seat. He never forgot the insult.

In 1907 the Transvaal government passed a law that all male Asians over the age of 8 had to register and carry a pass at all times. Gandhi led the protest against this law insisting it must be non violent. He called this Satyagraha. Many Indians were arrested. General Smuts, the Prime Minister, promised Gandhi the law would be repealed. He broke his word and over 2000 Indians burnt their passes in Johannnesburg. Eventually, the protests were successful and the law was repealed.

The Union

In 1908 white politicians proposed a union of the four colonies of South Africa. The British government wanted this because it was the best way of ensuring that the vast gold reserves in the Transvaal were safe for the Empire. To please the Afrikaners there was to be no extension of the Cape voting system to the rest of the Union. Each colony would operate under its old system. The Africans were in despair. They decided to send a delegation to England to petition the King and Parliament. A South African Convention was held at Bloemfontein in March 1909. Six delegates were chosen to go to London under the leadership of W. P. Schreiner, a white MP.

Source D The resolution passed by the South African Convention

That all persons in the Union should have full and equal rights . . . applicable alike to all citizens without distinction of class, colour or creed.

Source **E** shows how strange Schreiner's request was thought to be. He is standing beside King George V.

Source E Cartoon in Rand *Daily Mail*, 23 June 1909

Very few British MPs supported the Africans' demand. The Archbishop of Canterbury spoke in the House of Lords (Source **F**).

Source F The Archbishop of Canterbury, 16 August 1909

Natives will for generations to come be quite unfit to share equal citizenship with whites.

The Prime Minister, Herbert Asquith, said it was best to leave the problem to politicians in South Africa. The Union Bill became law in May 1910. The delegation had failed completely.

The new government

The first Prime Minister of the Union was Louis Botha, leader of the Afrikaners in the Boer War and his Deputy was Jan Christian Smuts, another war veteran. One of the first new laws in 1911 was the Mines and Works Act. It restricted non whites to menial jobs and fixed their pay at a small percentage of that for white men, treating Africans as second class citizens.

God bless Africa

Source G Nkosi Sikelel' *iAfrika*

The birth of a nation

This song is now the national anthem of South Africa. It was used in January 1912 when African leaders first met at Bloemfontein and formed the South African Native National Convention (later to be known as the ANC). It was to be a permanent organisation defending the freedom, rights and privileges of all African people.

Source H Pixley Ka Isaka Seme, Treasurer of the South African Native National Convention

We have discovered that in the land of their birth Africans are treated as hewers of wood and drawers of water. The white people of this country have formed what is known as the Union of South Africa – a Union in which we have no voice in the making of laws . . . we have therefore called this conference for the purpose of creating national unity and defending our rights.

Quoted in A. Odendaal, *Vukani Bantu!*, 1984

The Land Act

The Natives Land Act, passed in 1913, was even worse than the Mines Act. It banned all buying and selling of land between Africans and whites. Africans could be evicted from land they rented on white-owned farms and they were allocated land only in certain poor areas called 'Reserves'. Although the Africans were almost 70% of the total population they were allowed only 7% of the land (Source **J**).

It meant the destruction of African farming. It was decided to send another delegation to London to protest about the Act.

Source I Sol Plaatje, an African newspaper editor

The Boers are now ousting the Englishmen from the scene and when they have finished with them they will make a law declaring it a crime for a native to live in South Africa . . . from this it will be just one step to complete slavery.

From *Native Life in South Africa*, 1916

The delegation arrived in June 1914 (Source **K**). The King refused to see them. He said that Britain could not interfere in South African affairs. Then, in August 1914, war broke out. As loyal subjects of the King the Africans decided to end their protest, return home and offer their services to the government. It was to be a long time before they felt their African nationalism was stronger than their loyalty to the Empire.

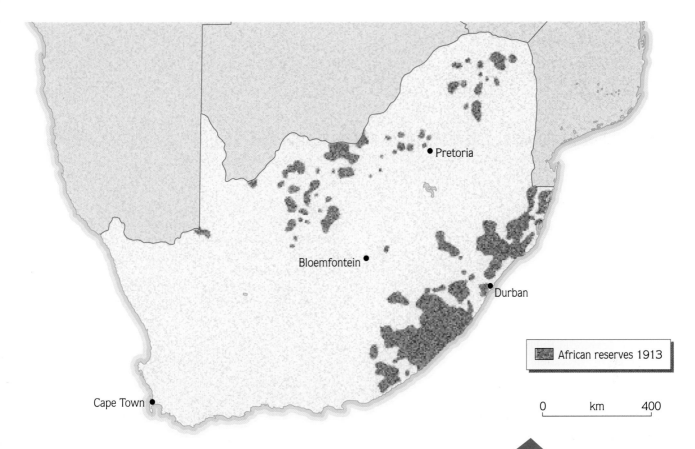

Source J African reserves in 1913

- Pretoria
- Bloemfontein
- Durban
- Cape Town

African reserves 1913

0   km   400

Source K The delegation to Britain (Left to right – Mapikela, Rubusana, Dube, Msane and Plaatje)

Questions

1 How many African, Indian and Coloured soldiers helped the British in the Boer War?

2 What did they hope for at the end of the war?

3 If Joseph Chamberlain thought the Peace treaty was shameful (Source **A**) why did he allow it to be signed?

4 Look at Sources **D** and **F** (page 21). Describe the different attitudes shown in the sources.

5 Does the cartoonist (Source **E**) think the King is taking the delegation seriously? Explain your answer.

6 Why do you think Africans call the meeting of the 'South African Native National Convention' in January 1912 'the birth of a nation' (Source **H**)?

7 Why do you think a delegation was sent to London in 1914, when the 1909 delegation failed?

4 Why apartheid?

Overview 1910–48

▶ **What were the key developments during these years?**

The Afrikaner rebellion

During the years 1910–48 most white politicians worked hard to bring the Afrikaans and English-speaking people closer together. They did not succeed completely. General Hertzog, the famous Boer War soldier left the government in 1912 and in 1914 formed the National Party for Afrikaners alone. When the Prime Minister, General Botha, decided to support the British Empire at the outbreak of war in 1914 nearly 10,000 Afrikaners rose in a rebellion which had to be put down by the army.

The Second World War and its aftermath

Hertzog became Prime Minister in 1924 and promoted Afrikaner interests in every possible way. At the outbreak of the Second World War in 1939 he resigned rather than support Britain. Smuts led South Africa into war on Britain's side. The war produced a sudden growth in the economy and new jobs in war industries. More than half a million blacks migrated to the cities. What would happen when they began to compete for jobs with whites after the war? Smuts admitted 'You might as well try to sweep the ocean back with a broom.'

Meanwhile, the response of African leaders to new race laws seemed remarkably moderate and cautious. They believed in non-violence, respect for the law, petitions and polite meetings with white leaders. A Pass burning campaign in 1930 (following Gandhi's example) collapsed after police killed the leader. Many black soldiers served in the army during the Second World War as non combatants. They expected that Smuts would recognise their loyalty by listening to their grievances. They were disappointed. They were even turned away from the Victory celebrations. Anton Lembede, one of the founders of the ANC Youth League in 1944, called the old men who led the ANC 'a body of gentlemen with clean hands'. He was determined to make changes.

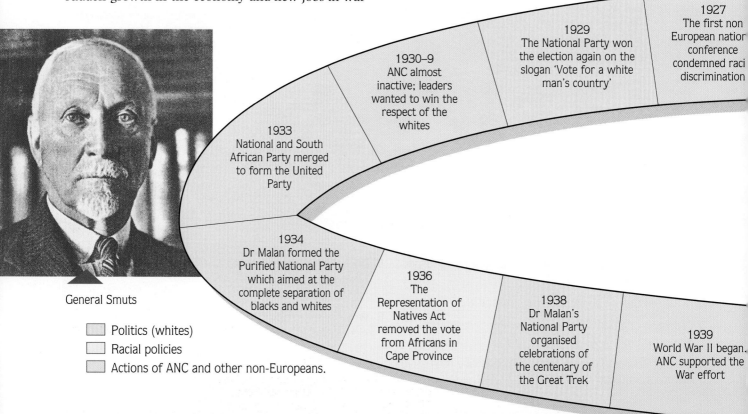

General Smuts

- Politics (whites)
- Racial policies
- Actions of ANC and other non-Europeans.

1927
The first non European nation conference condemned raci discrimination

1929
The National Party won the election again on the slogan 'Vote for a white man's country'

1930–9
ANC almost inactive; leaders wanted to win the respect of the whites

1933
National and South African Party merged to form the United Party

1934
Dr Malan formed the Purified National Party which aimed at the complete separation of blacks and whites

1936
The Representation of Natives Act removed the vote from Africans in Cape Province

1938
Dr Malan's National Party organised celebrations of the centenary of the Great Trek

1939
World War II began. ANC supported the War effort

General Hertzog

1910
Election won by South
African Party led by
Botha and Smuts

1914
ANC supported the
war effort; 5635
Africans died

1918
ANC petitioned King
George V to grant the
vote to Africans; he
refused

1918
White workers' wages on
Rand gold mines rose by
35%; African wages
remained the same

Reverend J. Calata,
Secretary of the ANC
1936–49

1922
Mine owners reduced
whites' wages; strikes
resulted – 250 whites
were killed

1923
Native Urban Areas
Act allowed towns to
build separate
locations for Africans

1924
Hertzog's National Party
won election and
promised 'to put whites
first and foremost'

1924
Thousands of
Africans were
sacked and
replaced by
'poor whites'

J. B. Marks, leader of
the mineworkers strike
1946

1940–5
The Afrikaner Ossewa
Brandwag opposed
the war effort and
sabotaged railways,
electricity and
telephones

1944
Lembede, Mandela,
Tambo and Sisulu formed
the ANC Youth League 'to
work for the freedom of
all Africans'

1946
50,000 African
miners went on
strike; police
killed 9 and
injured 1200

1948
Dr Malan's National
Party won the election.
Malan said 'South
Africa belongs to us
once more'

The National Party, Dr Malan and the Broederbond

▶ **How did Afrikaner nationalism develop?**

Source A The National Party Symbol. It represents a powder horn as used in the Boer War

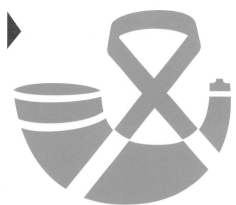

General Hertzog founded the National Party (Source **A**) in 1914 because he was worried that the Afrikaners would lose their identity in the new Union of South Africa.

Source B General Hertzog's speech at De Wildt, Transvaal in 1912

> I am not one of those who always have their mouths full of conciliation . . . South Africa must be governed by the Afrikaner.

In 1924 he became Prime Minister and set to work to remove all the disadvantages which he considered the Afrikaners had suffered since their defeat in the Boer War. As a start, Afrikaans was made an official language.

One of Hertzog's most energetic ministers was Dr Malan, a farmer's son whose family were neighbours of the Smuts. He had been a clergyman and later a newspaper editor. He was fanatical in his devotion to the Afrikaners.

> Afrikanerdom is not the work of men but the creation of God.
>
> **Quoted in Brian Lapping, *Apartheid, A History*, 1986**

Source C Dr Malan

A secret society

Malan remained in Hertzog's government until 1934 when he founded his own opposition party, the Purified National Party. Malan received great support from a secret all-male organisation called the Broederbond (Band of Brothers). It was the most secret political organisation in the world. The Broederbond was formed on 5 June 1918 when 14 Afrikaners met in a private house at 32 Marathon Street, Johannesburg

Source D The house where the Broederbond began

They decided to form a secret group to work together for the survival of the Afrikaner people. Dr Malan was one of the earliest members. Branches were formed all over the country and members promised to do everything in their power to help and promote the interests of fellow Afrikaners. They had their own special handshake to recognise one another, their own song and flag, and they never sent letters in case they were opened. By 1930 there were 500 members belonging to cells all over the country. Many of them recalled with bitterness the time their families had spent in Boer War concentration camps and their suffering in the Depression.

Source E   Chairman Piet Meyer's speech to Bondsraad, 1968

We were the Poor Whites, the Boers without markets and without capital; the lowly-paid, unskilled workers in mines and factories; we were the civil servants in the inferior jobs ... when the Great Depression came we were the first unemployed.

Their aim was always to help one another and eventually, members of the Broederbond rose to positions of power. Source **F** is part of a secret list of 1800 members.

Source F   A list of Broederbond members

GROENEWALD A.P.J., Farmer, Griekwastad	GREEFF P.D.I 1116
GOUWS J.J., Inspector, Worcester (Drosdy)	GEERTSEMA Pretoria, 91C
GROBBELAAR G.J., School Principal, Kimberley (Vooruitsig)	GROENEWAL 207
GOBREGTS C., Doctor, Bonnievale	GRIESEL J.D.
GELDENHUYS J.M., Farmer, Lichtenburg	GROBLER 6303
GROBBELAAR J.J., Doctor, Benoni	GROBLER
GOUWS D.J., Manager (Volkskas), Piet Retief	Potchetstroor
GOUGH J.P., Police, Greytown	GREEFF C.J.
GOUWS J.J., Police, Cape Town	GERBER P.
GROENEWALD H.J., Church Official, Trompsburg, 1095	GREYLING J. (Minister) Pre
GROENEWALD E.P., Professor, Pretoria, 2118	
GERMISHUYS J.A., Farmer, Heilbron, 2487	HOWARD W.I HEIGERS D. HOLTZHAUSE (Derdepoort)
GROBLER P.J., Civil Servant, Pretoria, 3023	

There was a special ceremony when a man joined the Bond. It always took place in a darkened room lit only by candles and arranged so the faces of the men around the walls were not visible. On the table the South African flag covered the Union Jack to represent the rejection of all things British (Source **G**). When an Afrikaner song had finished there was a reading from the Bible and the candidate was asked to swear an oath of secrecy.

Source G   A Broederbond table

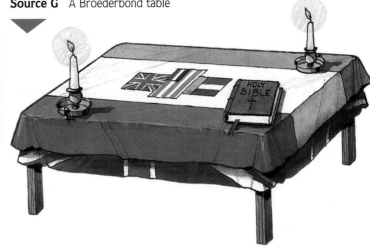

Source H   Part of the Broederbond initiation ceremony

The members of the Broederbond strive to represent and serve the best that is in our nation . . . to strive for the welfare and advancement of all people of the Afrikaner nation.

From J. Serfontein, *The Brotherhood of Power*, 1978

Finally, the candidate was asked whether he accepted the rules and, if he agreed, all members shook hands to confirm that he had joined.

Source I   The final words of the ceremony

He who betrays the Bond will be destroyed by the Bond. The Bond never forgets. Its vengeance is swift and sure.

From J Serfontein, *The Brotherhood of Power*, 1978

Questions

1 **a)** Why do you think the National Party chose a powder horn (Source **A**) as its symbol?
   b) How would you describe and explain Hertzog's attitude in Source **B**?

2 Using Source **C**, explain how the Afrikaners believed they were special.

3 What were the main aims of the Broederbond as indicated in Source **H**?

4 Study Sources **F**, **G**, **H** and **I**. Why did many people regard the Broederbond as a sinister organisation?

5 How far does Source **H** show that Hertzog's aim in Source **B** was being carried out?

Poor whites – problems and politics

Why did the poor whites feel so isolated?

The problem

South Africa was a land of promise and many white people made their fortunes easily. Inevitably some were not so successful. They were known as the 'poor whites'. They tended to be Afrikaners and suffered greatly after the Boer War and in the 1920s. Dr Malan came into contact with many poor white families in his work as a clergyman:

Source A   Speech made by Dr Malan to Church congress, 1910

I have observed the children of Afrikaner families running around as naked as kaffirs [an insulting word for 'natives'] in Congoland. We have knowledge today of Afrikaner girls so poor they work for coolies [unskilled labourers] and Chinese. These unfortunates are all our flesh and blood; they carry our names; they are Afrikaners, all of them.

Poor whites feared other whites looking down on them much the same as poor blacks – especially if they had to work for a black employer. They supported the idea of segregation – the separation of whites from blacks. It never occured to them that if poor whites and blacks protested together they might achieve some improvement.

Hertzog's actions

Hertzog made help for poor whites a top priority when he became Prime Minister in 1924. All government departments sacked so-called 'uncivilised' (black) workers and recruited 'civilised' whites in their place. The number of mining jobs reserved for 'whites' increased; 13,000 poor whites took over the jobs of blacks on the railways.

Economic depression in the 1920s and early 1930s brought further setbacks for poor whites.

By 1931 300,000 out of about one million Afrikaners were finding it very difficult to survive and make a living.

Source B   Evidence collected in an interview by Rev J. Albertyn for the Carnegie Report, 1932

My father was a landowner in Vanvhynsdorp but he lost all his stock owing to drought. For a time he took to transport riding. When I grew up, he and I took out a licence in Bushmanland and after a while we owned 1000 small cattle. But once more we lost nearly everything. I made one more attempt but the drought of 1913 ruined me completely – for twenty years I have had no fixed abode – the wagon is my home. My nine children were born while we were on trek.

In the countryside some poor whites even took jobs working for Africans – for them this was the ultimate shame.

Source C   Poor whites employed by black farmers

Finding jobs in town was even more difficult. Source **D** shows the number of white males unemployed in Johannesburg. Their familes lived in squalid slum conditions. They petitioned the Johannesburg town council in 1933 to provide better housing. The council's response was to move 30,000 Africans out of the city so they would not remind the poor whites how low they had sunk. The Broederbond tried to help by setting up a life assurance company and a bank in 1934.

Source D   Employment in Johannnesburg

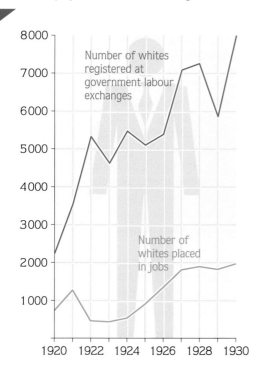

8000
7000
Number of whites registered at government labour exchanges
6000
5000
4000
3000
Number of whites placed in jobs
2000
1000

1920 1922 1924 1926 1928 1930

Source E   A digger's shack built of corrugated iron, canvas and hessian

Whenever a new discovery of gold or diamonds was announced the poor whites flocked to the mines (Sources **E** and **F**).

Source F   *The Star*, Johannesburg, 1925

Pitiful scenes of families living in squalor and misery; emaciated childen in rags which would be despised by houseboys [servants]; and careworn mothers trying to cook from scraps a frugal meal to enable dejected husbands to wrest precious stones from the earth with inadequate tools.

Quoted in Robert Morrell, *White But Poor*, 1992

One solution

Increasingly, the poor whites turned to the Purified National Party led by Dr Malan. He blamed the blacks for the whites' poverty and called for strict segregation. He appealed to Afrikaner nationalism. In 1938 Malan made a speech comparing competition for jobs with the Battle of Blood River which the trekkers fought and won in 1838.

Source G   Dr Malan's speech at the site of the Battle of Blood River, 1938

Your Blood River lies in the city . . . In that new Blood River black and white meet together in much closer contact and much more binding struggle than one hundred years ago . . . Today black and white jostle together in the labour market.

Apartheid was but a few steps away.

Questions

1 Look at Source **A**. What effect did Malan hope to have on his audience?

2 Is Source **C** reliable evidence for a person studying this topic? Give your reasons.

3 Explain the meaning of the phrase 'despised by houseboys' in Source **F**.

4 Explain why you think Dr Malan compared competition for jobs in 1938 with the Battle of Blood river in 1838 (Source **G**).

Myths and legends – the justification of apartheid

How did the Afrikaners develop the myth of the Covenant?

Afrikaners often talked about their destiny, the purity of their blood and God's special protection over them.

Source A From the *New Illustrated History for the Senior Certificate*, 1969

> On December 9 1838 they . . . made a Covenant that, if God should deliver their enemies into their hands, they would erect a House of Worship to the glorification of His name and the day would always be observed as a Sabbath – until the last generation.

A covenant means a solemn promise made between God and a group of people as in the Bible stories. This story is part of the history of the Great Trek (see page 14 and Source **B**).

Source B Wagons descending Mackay's Nek

In December 1838 Andries Pretorius led an attack on the Zulus. On the night of 15 December the Afrikaners made a laager [a camp in a circle of waggons] on the bank of the Ncome river. The next day at dawn a Zulu army of 10,000 launched an attack. Their shields and assegais [iron-tipped spears] were no match for guns and cannons. The Zulus left 3000 dead. The Afrikaners had not lost a single man. They named it the Battle of Blood River because the water was stained with so much Zulu blood. Perhaps this victory was the proof of the covenant they had made with God.

But what is the evidence? Andries Pretorius wrote an account of the battle on 23 December 1838. He did not mention a covenant or a promise to celebrate the anniversary of the victory. The early histories of the battle did not mention the promise. So how did the myth that the Afrikaners were God's chosen people develop?

In 1876 Sarel Cilliers' Journal was published. He was a church leader who had been present with Pretorius. He wrote his journal nearly 40 years after the events he described,

Source C From H. J. Hotstede, *Geschiedenis van den Oranjie-Vrijstaat*, 1876

. . . I took my place on a gun carriage. my words were these: 'My Brethren and fellow-countrymen, at this moment we stand before the holy God of heaven and earth to make a promise if He will be with us and protect us and deliver the enemy into our hands . . . that we shall observe the day and the date as an anniversary in each year

Political use of the myth

Then the politicians took over. In 1880 President Kruger of the Transvaal ordered that 16 December should be a public holiday in memory of the promise. He wanted to encourage the belief that the Afrikaners were God's chosen people. The myth grew stronger over the years. In 1938 it was decided to build a monument to celebrate the centenary of the Great Trek. A panel entitled 'The Taking of the Vow' was to be the central feature (Source **D**)

Source D The Vow panel in the Voortrekker Monument

More than 100,000 Afrikaners attended the laying of the foundation stone of the Voortrekker monument (Source **E**).

The leader of the National Party, Dr Malan, made a speech (Source **F**).

Source F

They received their task from God's Hand. They gave their answer. They made their sacrifices. There is still a white race . . . Will South Africa still be a white man's country at the end of this century?

From Du Toit and Steenkamp, *Eeufees-Gedenboek*, 1938

What happened when the myth was challenged?

In March 1979 a South African historian, Professor van Jaarsveld, dared question the story of the Covenant. He made it known that he had a new interpretation of the Battle of Blood River which he would explain in a public lecture.

Source G *Sunday Times*, 1 April 1979, Johannesburg

. . . a gang of about 40 burly men burst into the hall, surrounded van Jaarsveld, emptied a tin of tar over him and plastered him with feathers. During the assault a man who identified himself as Eugene Terreblanche seized the microphone . . . [and said] 'Professor van Jaarsveld attacks the sanctity of the Afrikaner in his deepest essence . . . this standpoint is blasphemous [insulting of someone's beliefs].

Source E The Voortrekker monument

Questions

1 Why is the story of the Great Trek so important to many Afrikaners?

2 Is Source **C** reliable? Give your reasons.

3 Design a poster explaining why Afrikaners should give money to build the monument in 1938.

4 When Nelson Mandela became President in 1994, why do you think he spoke about the *new* covenant?

5 The creation of the apartheid state 1948–55

The General Election 1948

 Why was 1948 a turning point and what was put in place?

In May 1948 there was a General Election. Smut's United Party fought Malan's National Party. Smuts had already been Prime Minister for 14 years. Malan was regarded as an outsider.

Source A   Dr Malan and his wife in 1948

Source B   Rose Jordan, an English woman living in Cape Town

Dr Malan has coined a new catchword for his election slogan – 'Apartheid' which represents his declared policy of compulsorily segregating the coloured and native population from the Europeans . . . This scheme is getting him into some difficulties. The United Party points to the absolute necessity of employing native and coloured labour in the factories. It is economically out of the question to move the non-Europeans to distant districts . . .

From *The Guardian*, 25 May 1948

Apartheid means apartness. Dr Malan used the word because it described exactly his party's policy of separating blacks and whites into distinct areas. He said that people would have rights only in their own areas. There was nothing new about this idea of separation or segregation. Most politicians in South Africa supported it. What was different in 1948 was that Malan intended to put his policies into practice, ruthlessly and comprehensively. The races must be separated in all spheres of life.

The effects of apartheid

Politicians in the past had never put their segregation policies fully into practice. Black workers were needed in the factories, so forced segregation would be an economic disaster. Black servants were needed in the houses of rich white people, so they had to live in the towns.

Dr Malan used another slogan in the election – 'swart gevaar' which means black peril. He recognised that many whites in the cities were worried about crime, rising prices and white unemployment. An easy answer to their worries was to blame the blacks. He told the whites that if the blacks were forced into separate areas the problems would melt away. He also blamed the communists for causing problems.

Source C   Speech made by Dr Malan at Paarl, 20 April, 1948

Will the European race in the future be able to maintain its rule, its purity and its civilisation or will it float along until it vanishes for ever in the Black sea of South Africa? Will the all destroying Communist cancer be checked? The Native reserves must be retained . . . Natives in Europeans areas can make no claim to political rights . . .

Source D   The first Afrikaner cabinet, 1948

Source E   Cartoon in the *Daily Mail*

The result of the General Election

To the surprise of many people, the National Party won an overall majority of five. Dr Malan called it 'a miracle of God'. At last the Afrikaners who formed only 12% of the population had won control of the country. Dr Malan formed the first all-Afrikaner government. There were no politicians of British descent in his cabinet (Source **D**) and they all spoke Afrikaans at their meetings.

Dr Malan was determined to show he meant business. Within the first week he told his Minister of Transport to arrange for some carriages in all trains to be allocated for 'whites only'. It was a small beginning.

Over the next five years Malan's government organised the passing of laws to set up an apartheid state (Source **F** on page 34). Some people believed they were storing up trouble for the future (Source **E**).

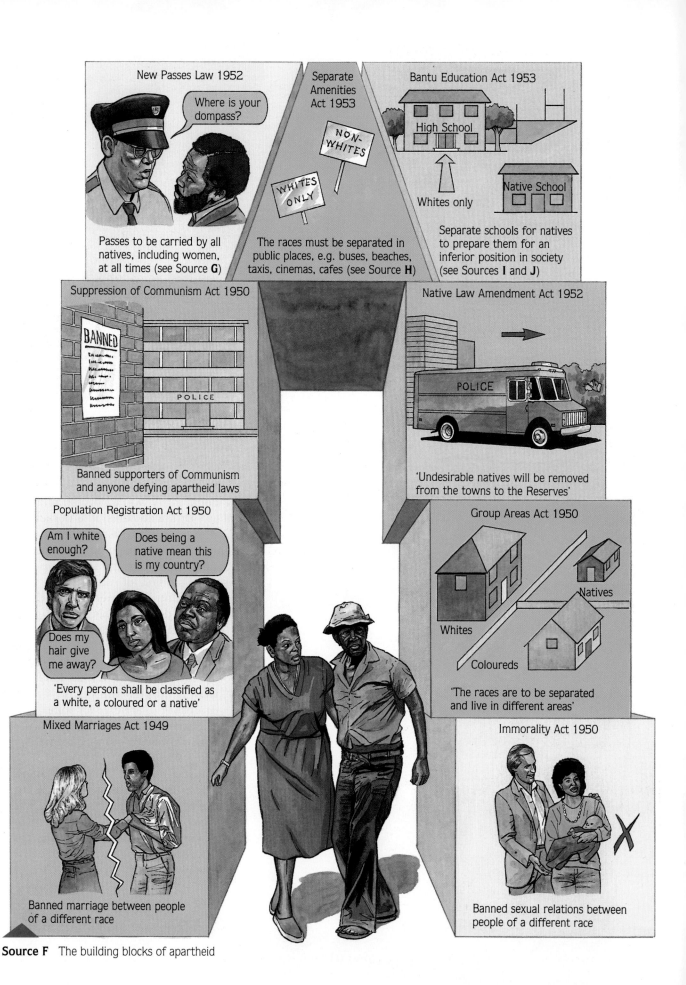

Source F The building blocks of apartheid

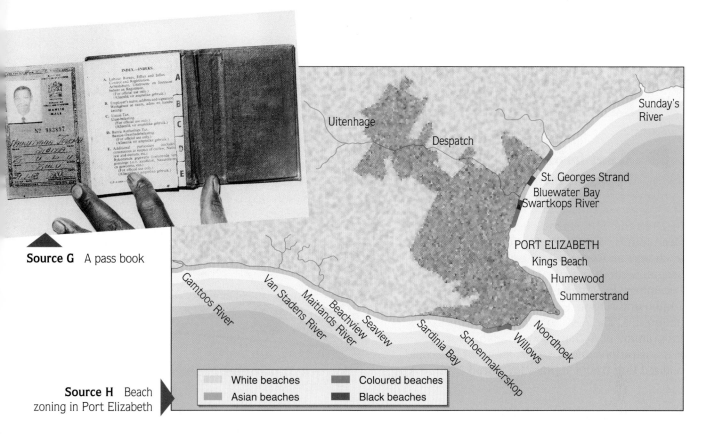

Source G A pass book

Source H Beach zoning in Port Elizabeth

Map labels: Uitenhage, Despatch, Sunday's River, St. Georges Strand, Bluewater Bay, Swartkops River, PORT ELIZABETH, Kings Beach, Humewood, Summerstrand, Gamtoos River, Van Stadens River, Maitlands River, Beachview, Seaview, Sardinia Bay, Schoenmakerskop, Willows, Noordhoek

White beaches / Asian beaches / Coloured beaches / Black beaches

Schools under apartheid

Before apartheid most schools for Africans were run by foreign missionaries but the government thought their influence might be dangerous so they were closed. Dr Hendrik Verwoerd became Minister of Native Affairs, and his new law, called the Bantu Education Act (1953), made syllabuses in African schools different from those in white schools. Government Inspectors carefully checked the books to make sure teachers taught the 'correct' facts.

Source I Speech by Dr Verwoerd in Parliament, 1954

The natives will be taught from childhood to realise that equality with Europeans is not for them . . .

Teachers in Cape Town used to joke that they had two sets of notes for History lessons – one was for exam purposes and Inspection visits, and the other was headed, 'The Truth'. Nevertheless, many lessons seemed strange to African children.

Source J From Z. K. Matthews, *Freedom For My People*, 1981

Our history, as we absorbed it from the tales and talk of our elders bore no resemblance to South African history as it is taught in South African schools . . . Yet we had to give back in exam papers the answers the white man expected.

Questions

1 What is the meaning of apartheid?

2 Was the idea of apartheid completely new in 1948? Explain your answer.

3 Look at Source **F**. Why do you think the Population Registration Act came before the Group Areas Act?

4 Source **E** is a reaction to the laws of apartheid (Source **F**). What do you think is the message of the cartoon?

5 Did African children believe the whites' version of South African history they had to learn in school (Source **J**)? Explain your answer.

6 In groups, use what you have read so far in this chapter to make up and perform a short play which explains what apartheid meant from the different points of view of the following:
  • Europeans who supported apartheid,
  • Europeans who broke apartheid laws,
  • Africans, Indians and Coloureds.

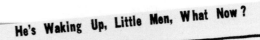
He's Waking Up, Little Men, What Now?

What forms did opposition take?

In 1948 the ANC was still led by 'gentlemen with clean hands'. The Youth League was determined to change all that. Walter Sisulu of the Youth League became Secretary-General of the ANC in December 1949 and a few weeks later Oliver Tambo and Nelson Mandela joined the Executive Committee. The ANC soon adopted the League's Programme of Action. It was a plan for strikes, demonstrations and boycotts. Some white people realised that troubled times lay ahead (Source **A**).

Source A Cartoon from the South African *Guardian*, 19 March 1950

Source B From a wall poster in 1950

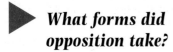

NATIONAL DAY OF PROTEST AND MOURNING

FOR ALL THOSE WHO HAVE LOST THEIR LIVES IN THE STRUGGLE FOR LIBERATION IN SOUTH AFRICA

Stay At Home

On

Monday 26 June 1950

From Karis and Carter, *From Protest to Challenge*, 1973

However, before the ANC could organise a national campaign the Transvaal ANC joined the Indian Congress and the Communist Party to plan a general strike for 1 May 1950. Mandela and other leaders opposed the strike, They did not want to co-operate with anyone who was not an ANC member. Nevertheless, the strike was a great success except that the police killed 18 African demonstrators at Orlando West. In reaction to these murders, the ANC, along with the Indians and the Communists, organised a National Day of Protest and Mourning for 26 June (Source **B**). It was a turning point. Mandela admitted that everyone who suffered under apartheid laws had to stand and fight together.

Despite all this co-operation, protest groups were still far from united. In May 1951 the government's proposal to remove the right to vote from Coloured people in the Cape led to demonstrations in front of Parliament by men carrying flaming torches. These men who had fought in the Second World War called themselves the Torch Commando. They lost support after a few months without achieving anything.

The defiance campaign

In 1951 the ANC and the Indian Congress decided to organise members to break the apartheid laws and to provoke the police to arrest them. They followed the example of Mahatma Gandhi (see pages 20–1) and decided there must be no violence. Mandela was made chairman of the Action Committee. The campaign started on 26 June 1952, the anniversary of the Day of Protest and Mourning, renamed Freedom Day.

Source C   Another wall poster in 1950

FORWARD TO FREEDOM IN 1952

This year 1952 marks three hundred years since, under Jan van Riebeeck, the first white people came to live in South Africa. The Malan Government is using this occasion to celebrate everything in South African history that glorifies the conquest, enslavement and oppression of the Non-European people.

IT IS TIME TO PUT AN END TO SLAVERY IN SOUTH AFRICA
We demand the right to live as human beings
We want the right to vote

THIS IS A CALL TO EVERY MAN AND WOMAN TO JOIN THE STRUGGLE FOR FREEDOM

From Karis and Carter, *From Protest to Challenge*, 1973

The campaign began in Port Elizabeth where 33 protesters entered a railway station through the WHITES ONLY door. They were arrested. Others asked to be served at White counters in Post Offices (Source **D**), broke the Pass Laws and sang 'Hi Malan, open the jail doors, we want to get in'. Mandela led a group of 52 men to break the law by walking in a Whites Only area of Johannesburg in the late evening. Every day newspapers carried pictures of black people defying the apartheid laws (Sources **E** and **F**)

The Police arrested over 8000 volunteers who refused to pay fines. The prisons were overflowing. However, the government refused to change its policies and by the end of the year ANC leaders called off the campaign. Despite this Mandela said that at last he felt he had come of age as a freedom fighter.

Source D   Plan of a segregated Post Office

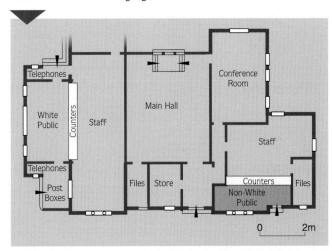

Source E   Africans defying apartheid in trains, 1952

Source F   A demonstration in Johannesburg

The Freedom Charter

Albert Lutuli: key dates

*c.*1898	born at Bulawayo, Rhodesia (Zimbabwe)
1908	Family returned to Natal
1918	trained as a teacher
1921–36	teacher at Adams College, Durban
1936	elected chief of Abasemakholweni tribe
1945	joined ANC
1952	elected president of the ANC banned for 4 years
1956	arrested and charged with High Treason
1957	released after a year in detention
1959	banned for 5 years
1960	burned his Pass in public
1961	awarded Nobel Peace Prize
1967	killed in a railway accident

Source G Wolfie Kodesh, interviewed in 1989

I remember going into the countryside . . . we got answers from women, children, farm workers, the whole lot. We even got ideas written on the back of Cavalla cigarette boxes, pieces of cardboard or paper. It was a very difficult task because people were not used to expressing themselves openly.

Quoted in Pampallis, *Foundations of the New South Africa*, 1991

In December 1952 the ANC elected Albert Lutuli as President. He supported the proposal to hold a Congress of the People. At this Congress delegates would decide the sort of country they wanted the new South Africa to be. The ANC worked closely with the Indians, the Coloureds and a group of white supporters to plan the meeting. Over 200 organisations were involved. Local committees all over the country asked people: 'How would you set about making South Africa a happy place for all the people who live in it?' (Source **G**).

The Congress was held at Kliptown near Johannesburg on 26 June 1955. Many leaders were not able to attend because of banning orders. Despite police road blocks nearly 3000 people (320 Indians, 230 Coloured, 112 whites and 2300 Africans) were there to listen to the Freedom Charter read to them in English, Sesotho and Xhosa. Every white person was photographed by the police. The crowd adopted the Charter by shouting its approval to each section with the word, 'Afrika'. The Freedom Charter became one of the most important documents in South African history. It demanded a non racial South Africa with political rights for all regardless of race, colour or sex; a fair distribution of wealth and the right to education and social security for all.

Source H   Part of the crowd who adopted the Freedom Charter

We, the people of South Africa, declare for all our country and the world to know;

That South Africa belongs to all who live in it, black and white, and that no government can justly claim authority unless it is based on the will of the people;

That our people have been robbed of their birthright to land, liberty and peace by a form of government founded on injustice and inequality;

That our country will never be prosperous or free until all our people live in brotherhood, enjoying equal rights and opportunities;

That only a democratic state based on the will of the people, can secure to all their birthright without distinction of colour, race, sex or belief;

And therefore, we the people of South Africa, black and white, together equals, countrymen and brothers, adopt this Freedom Charter. And we pledge ourselves to strive together, sparing nothing of our strength and courage, until the democratic changes set out here have been won.

Source I   An extract from the Freedom Charter

Questions

1   Look at Source **A**.
   a) Why do you think the black man is shown as a giant and what are being used to tie him down?
   b) What events in 1950 proved the cartoonist was correct in his prediction that the Black man was waking up (Source **B**)?

2   What was special to both Europeans and Non Europeans about June 1952 (Source **C**)?

3   How were the ANC leaders able to claim the Freedom Charter really did come from the people (Sources **G** and **H**)?

4   Put yourself in the place of a government minister reading the Freedom Charter (Source **I**). Write a comment from his point of view.

Bishop Trevor Huddleston

▶ *Why is he remembered in the struggle against apartheid?*

Source A Trevor Huddleston in Sophiatown

Source B Desmond Tutu, Archbishop of Cape Town and winner of the Nobel Peace Prize, remembers meeting Trevor Huddleston

▼

The very first time I met him was when I was a boy of about 8 or 9. We were standing with my mother on the balcony when this white man in a big black hat and a white flowing cassock swept past . . . You could have knocked me down with a feather, young as I was at the time, when this man doffed his hat to my mother; I couldn't understand a white man doffing his hat to a black woman, an uneducated woman . . .

From D. Honoré, *Essays on Huddleston*, 1988

Eleven universities have honoured this man by giving him degrees. The United Nations awarded him their Gold Medal. The African National Congress gave him the Isitwalandwe, the highest award they can give to anyone, 'for outstanding service in the cause of South Africa's freedom'.

Yet Trevor Huddleston is not a politician or a soldier. He is simply a monk who worked in South Africa and had the courage to stand up to apartheid. He became famous for writing a best-selling book in which he described his experiences in South Africa.

Source C Trevor Huddleston, *Naught For Your Comfort*, 1956

▼

I could tell you the story of Jonas . . . who was arrested one morning and charged with being a vagrant . . . by the time I reached the police station he was waiting in the yard before being locked up for the night. 'Where is your Pass?' I asked him. 'They tore it up'. Luckily the waste-paper basket was still there: luckily I found the Pass in four pieces. And when I refused to surrender it to the sergeant I was arrested myself. But at least I had the satisfaction a few days later of a complete apology – yet for every boy like Jonas whose arrest was reported to me there are thousands who have no one to care: a thousand for whom a torn up Pass might mean ten days in prison, the loss of a job, the beginning of that swift and terrible journey into crime.

The South African government banned the book. A large part of it tells the story of the destruction of Sophiatown near Johannesburg (Source **D**). Thousands of black people lived in Sophiatown where many owned homes and land. To put apartheid into practice the government decided to move the people and destroy their homes with bulldozers. Father Huddleston tried to stop this from happening.

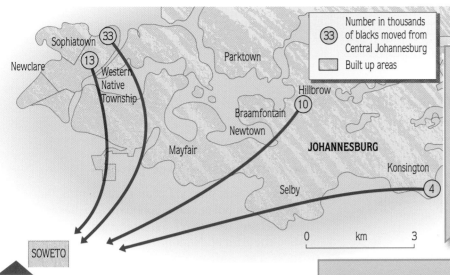

Source D   The moving of black people from Johannesburg

header CASE FILE

source D map

source E

source F

source G

questions

key dates

Source E   Trevor Huddleston, *Naught For Your Comfort*

9 February 1955 . . . a whole fleet of army lorries was drawn up . . . lining the street were thousands of police . . . a few Sten guns were in position at various points . . . Already the lorries were piled high with the pathetic possessions which had come from the row of rooms in the background . . .

Source F   The government's version of events

The Rev. Trevor Huddleston formed the Protest committee which tried its best to incite the Blacks to rebellion. Yet on the day of the great move everything was calm . . . many rejoiced at escaping from living conditions that had been insufferable . . .

From the entry for Hendrick Verwoerd in the *Dictionary of South African Biography*, 1981

In 1955 Huddleston had to leave South Africa. However, this did not stop him telling the world about apartheid and leading many campaigns outside South Africa to end it (Source **G**).

Source G   Campaigning against apartheid in 1985

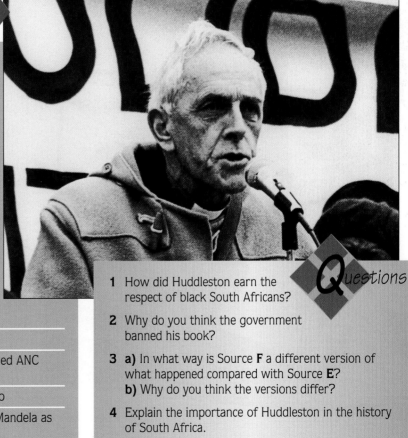

Trevor Huddleston: key dates

1913	born in Bedford
1937	became a priest
1941	became a monk
1943	priest in charge of Sophiatown
1955	left South Africa
1956	published *Naught For Your Comfort*
1959	founder member of the Anti-Apartheid Movement
1960	Bishop in Africa
1968	Bishop in London
1981	President of the Anti-Apartheid Movement
1982	launched campaign to free Mandela
1991	made opening speech at first unbanned ANC Conference
1993	took funeral service for Oliver Tambo
1994	attended inauguration of President Mandela as his personal guest.

Questions

1 How did Huddleston earn the respect of black South Africans?

2 Why do you think the government banned his book?

3 a) In what way is Source **F** a different version of what happened compared with Source **E**?
   b) Why do you think the versions differ?

4 Explain the importance of Huddleston in the history of South Africa.

6 Separate development in a police state

The second phase of apartheid

> ### ▶ How did Dr Verwoerd make apartheid work?

Dr Verwoerd became Prime Minister in September 1958. He was confident that his apartheid policy was the answer to all the country's problems. It simply needed completion and ruthless enforcement.

Source A From a broadcast by Dr Verwoerd, 2 September 1958

> Full opportunity for all can only be planned and achieved for everyone within his own racial community.

The last major brick in the apartheid wall was the Bantu Self Government Act passed in 1959 (page 46). The intention was that the people in the Bantustans should gradually learn to govern themselves. Transkei was the first Bantustan to become self-governing in 1963. Source **B** shows what the cartoonist of the *Cape Times* thought of this.

Source B 'It works!'

Courtesy of *The Cape Times*

The increase of police powers

Enforcement was simply a process of turning the country into a police state. Following clashes with the police in 1960 (see pages 54–5) the government banned the African National Congress (ANC) and its rival, the Pan African Congress (PAC). Police powers dramatically increased: they had the power to detain suspects without charge for 12 days (1962), then for 90 days (1963) and for 180 days (1965). Reports of torture in detention became common. The first prisoner to die in detention was L. Ngudle on 5 September 1963. The police claimed he hanged himself. His death was the first of many for which the police announced causes which few people believed. Their frustration is expressed in the following poem:

Source C

> He slipped on a piece of soap while washing
> He hanged himself
> He slipped on a piece of soap while washing
> He fell from the ninth floor
> He hanged himself while washing
> He slipped from the ninth floor
> He hung from the ninth floor
> He slipped on the ninth floor while washing
> He fell from a piece of soap while slipping
> He hung from the ninth floor
> He washed from the ninth floor while slipping
> He hung from a piece of soap while washing
>
> **Christopher van Wyk, *South African Freedom Poems*, 1980**

Banning orders were everyday occurrences – a banned person could not attend any meetings, write, broadcast or move from home without police permission. The police harassed newspaper reporters. The law forbade newspapers to quote a banned person. A Publications Board rigidly enforced censorship. To help the police the Active Citizen Force (founded in 1912) recruited more members. No stone was left unturned to make apartheid work.

What was it like to live in the apartheid state?

Apartheid affected every aspect of life in South Africa. It went further than signs on park benches, public toilets, buses, shops, restaurants, cinemas and beaches which reserved them for 'whites' or 'blacks' only. Apartheid also meant separation of the 'races' in education, jobs, places to live, hospitals. In 1965 the *Cape Times* drew attention to the pettiness of apartheid by publishing a list of small incidents (Source **D**).

Apartheid created unfairness and inequality and led to an increase in crime. For the South African economy which depended on a mostly non-white work force apartheid created problems. Living apart meant greater distances to travel to work. White women worried about finding black servants to do their housework and look after their children.

Black people could only watch rugby at Newlands B ground if there was a 6 feet high wire fence to separate them from other spectators.

A blind white girl could not travel in the same taxi as her black maid.

A United States aircraft carrier could only dock in Cape Town harbour if the pilots were white.

Judges of a Coloured Beauty Contest at Paarl could not be white.

Source D 'The pinpricks of apartheid' from the *Cape Times*, 1965

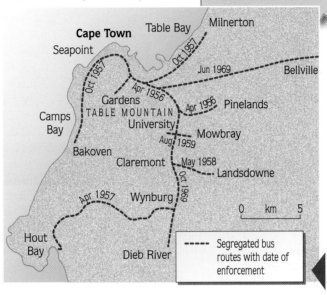

No detail was too small to escape the government's attention. In every city buses were segregated.

Source E Segregated bus routes in Cape Town

Living conditions

Apartheid forced most Africans to live in poverty in the richest country in Africa; a country which was becoming even richer because the economy was rapidly expanding. Over a million Africans lived in Soweto, a township created on the edge of Johannesburg in the 1950s to house people moved from places like Sophiatown (see page 41) which were too close to whites.

Soweto covers 85 square kilometres. 108,766 red or grey brick houses are built opposite each other in straight rows. Most homes use candles, paraffin or gas lamps for lighting. Coal stoves are used in almost all the homes. Only a quarter of the houses in Soweto have running cold water inside the house. The majority have outside taps. Only three houses in a hundred have hot water, only seven in a hundred have a bath or a shower.

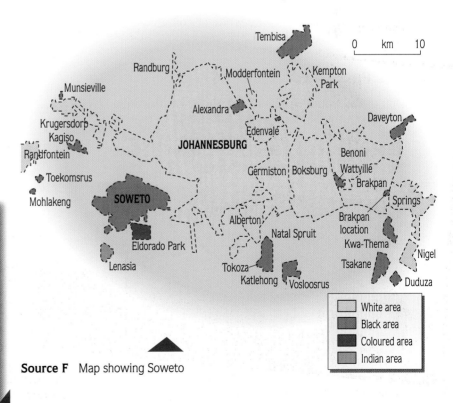

Source F Map showing Soweto

Source G From Joyce Sikakane, *Window on Soweto*, 1976

43

People who lived in Soweto had a shorter journey to work in Johannesburg than many others who lived too far away to travel there daily. These workers lived in migrant hostels and returned to see their families for only one month each year. Source **H** shows a room which was home to twenty-five migrant workers. Each shelf, made of concrete, was one man's living space for up to a year.

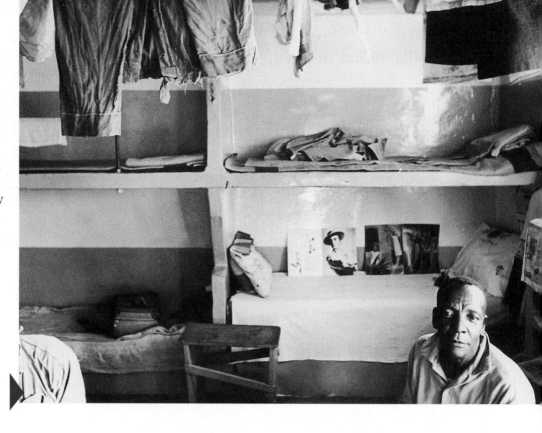

Source H Inside a migrant hostel in 1970

No one escaped

Apartheid created employment for a vast army of minor 'officials' – civil servants recruited from the better educated 'poor whites'. One young unmarried Afrikaner woman recorded her meeting with an official at the Population Registration Office. He had to decide whether her baby was pure white or coloured before it could be adopted (Source **I**).

The Pass Laws

One of the worst aspects of apartheid was the daily harassment of blacks by the police to check their passes. No black person without special permission could stay in a white area for more than 72 hours. Passes had to be carried at all times.

Source I Quoted in Peter Lambley, *The Psychology of Apartheid*, 1980

I had to wait in this corridor with the baby . . . After an age, I was ushered into this horrid little man's room . . . He looked at me with a sneer . . . He wanted to know everything. About me, the birth, the baby, about David, the father – everything. He wrote it all down. . . . He treated me like criminal – worse . . . It all seemed so crazy. Then this pig grilled me about when it all happened. 'Are you sure,' he says, 'that David is the father? I mean,' he sits back with a leer, 'given your behaviour, it could be anyone.' I had to tell him who else I had been out with and how far we went. Then he wanted to know about the time when David and I had intercourse, whether he had ejaculated or not . . . He wanted to know where it was, whether it was in the middle of my period or not. I could tell he was getting a real kick out of this . . . Him with his pictures of his wife and four children on the desk next to him. Then he asks me to stand up and looks at me hard, carnally. Looks especially at my face and my skin colour and my hair and texture. Then he asks about David and his colour. Last he looks at the baby and examines its face, hair and finger-nails. He takes out a book with pictures of babies in it, head sizes, figures, profiles and compares the baby's with it. Then he lets me go.

Source J An officer examining a pass book

In one typical year, 1962, there were 384,497 convictions under the Pass Laws (Source **K**).

Source K You are all under arrest!

Forced removals

Between 1951 and 1986 at least four million people were forced to move from white areas to Bantustans and black townships on the edge of white towns (Source **L**).

Black people who had lived in Kenton-on-Sea for twenty-five years were given just eleven days notice of their removal to the Ciskei Bantustan (Source **M**).

Source L A woman in despair as she is moved to Soweto in 1955

Source M Report in the *City Press*, Johannesburg, 1964

We are being dumped here very much against our will – only to die. People are starving . . . You only find five people at a service because they are hungry and do not have enough energy to go to church.

Questions

1 Explain the meaning of the cartoon (Source **B**, page 42).

2 How does the poem (Source **C**, page 42) suggest that police reports were not trustworthy?

3 Why do you think the *Cape Times* published examples of 'pinprick' apartheid (Source **D**, page 43)?

4 If people complained about conditions in Soweto (Source **G**, page 43) what might the government reply?

5 The government banned publication of the photographs in Sources **H** and **L**.
   a) Why do you think this was?
   b) Why are they useful to historians?

6 What needs to be checked to prove that Source **I** is reliable?

7 What point is the cartoonist making in Source **K**? How is it useful to an historian?

Dr Hendrik Verwoerd

Why is he known as 'the architect of apartheid'?

Hendrik Verwoerd: key dates

1901	born near Amsterdam in Holland.
1903	family emigrated to South Africa.
1924	lecturer in psychology at Stellenbosch University, later Professor
1927	married Betsie Schoombe; eight children
1941	High Court Judge declared he was a Nazi supporter
1948	entered Parliament
1950	Minister of Native Affairs
1958	Prime Minister
1959	Bantu Self-Government Act
1961	South Africa became a Republic
1966	assassinated

Source A   Albert Lutuli, *Let My People Go*, 1962

> If any one man is remembered as the author of our calamity it will be he.

Source B   Speech by Dr Verwoerd in Parliament, 3 September 1948

> Nobody will deny that for the Native as well as for the European, complete separation would have been the ideal. If the Native had not had anything to do with the whites, if he was capable of managing his own affairs it would have been ideal.

Verwoerd was a fanatic and a workaholic. He refused to listen to his critics. Harold Macmillan, the British Prime Minister, visited South Africa in 1960.

Source C   Harold Macmillan, *Pointing the Way*, 1972

> I had long discussions with Dr Verwoerd . . . Apartheid to him was . . . a religion . . . I had the unusual experience of soon noticing that nothing one could say would have the smallest effect upon this determined man . . . it was a blank wall.

Bantustans

In 1959 Verwoerd had a law passed to create separate homelands for Africans or, as he preferred to call them, Bantus. In these Bantustans (Source **D**) black people would have their own government but they would not be completely independent. The white South African government would still control defence and foreign policy. Verwoerd said it would be at least 2000 years before the Bantus were ready for real independence. It followed from this policy that blacks in white areas were now just visitors with no rights and could expect to be 'returned' to their homelands.

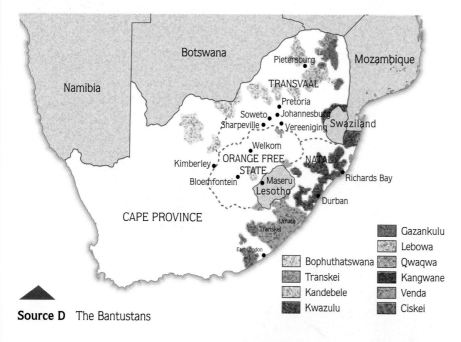

Source D   The Bantustans

The Republic of South Africa

In 1961 Verwoerd took great pleasure in cutting South Africa's last link with Britain and making South Africa a republic. Before he did so he held a referendum [a nationwide vote] for those who had the right to vote to see if there was support for the idea. Some 850,488 voted in favour; 775,878 voted against.

Assassination

On 6 September 1966 Verwoerd was sitting in the South African Parliament when he was approached by a European messenger, Demetrio Tsafandas.

Source E The assassination of the Prime Minister

[T]safandas] swiftly pulled out a knife and threw himself upon the Prime Minister. In quick succession, he stabbed his victim four times on the neck and chest. At first, Verwoerd smiled, thinking the messenger had stumbled on him by accident, and trying to indicate by his smile that it did not matter. Then his expression changed as he saw the blood on his chest.

From H. Kenney, *Architect of Apartheid*, 1980

The assassin's motive for killing Verwoerd was not political. Tsafandas claimed that a tapeworm in his stomach, put there by the devil, had driven him to do it. Verwoerd received a hero's burial. Those who had looked up to him built a statue of him (Source **F**) as a mark of their respect. However, not all Afrikaners admired him (Source **G**).

Source F Statue of Verwoerd

Source G An Afrikaner businessman speaking about Verwoerd

He wasn't a real Afrikaner like the rest of us – he tried too hard to be an Afrikaner and really, despite all his brains, he got it wrong. Let's face it, would you, being honest, believe in apartheid and all that bullshit he came up with? No one does. . . . We know sooner or later we'll be stopped, we've just been very lucky to get away with it for so long . . . We trusted him, man, thinking he was just like us. But he wasn't. Like Hitler maybe, like all those wartime Afrikaners. Thank God somebody stopped him before it was too late.

Quoted in Lambley, *The Psychology of Apartheid*, 1980

Questions

1 What impression of Verwoerd did those who built his statue (Source **F**) want to give?

2 What aim does Source **B** tell us that Verwoerd was working towards?

3 The businessman quoted in Source **G** was speaking from memory in 1979.
   a) If he was correct why do you think Verwoerd lasted in power so long?
   b) As historians what questions would you have asked this witness if you had been interviewing him?

4 Draw a labelled diagram or a poster or a cartoon to illustrate why Verwoerd is remembered as 'the architect of Apartheid'.

7 How opposition to apartheid developed 1955–64

Overview

► ## What different forms did opposition to apartheid take?

The South African Communist Party played an important part in bringing together the multi-racial alliance which produced the Freedom Charter of 1955. The Nationalist Government saw this alliance as a serious threat and blamed communist Russia.

Source A From W. J. de Kock's *History of South Africa*, published by the South African Government, 1971

In 1956 the Russian Consulate [the building lived in by those sent by Russia to protect the interests of her people overseas] in Pretoria, which was known to be causing unrest among Non-Whites, was closed down, and the police arrested a large number of persons on charges of high treason in 1956.

The state of emergency

The so-called Treason Trial (page 49) lasted from 1956–61 and in the end found all the accused 'not guilty'. Meanwhile, resistance to the intolerable conditions created by apartheid laws continued (Source **B**). Frustration at lack of progress by the Freedom Charter alliance led to a split in the ANC in 1959 and the setting up of a rival organisation, the Pan African Congress (PAC). Then in 1960 the PAC organised a demonstration against the Pass Laws in the township of Sharpeville. The police opened fire and shot dead 69 Africans and wounded 180. From around the world there was a storm of protest against the action of the police. The South African Prime Minister, Verwoerd, declared a State of Emergency and banned the ANC, PAC and Communist Party. A lawyer and an ANC leader, Nelson Mandela, formed Umkhonto we Sizwe (The Spear of the Nation, also known as MK, see pages 56–7). MK was a guerilla organisation which planned to use sabotage, and if necessary terrorism to overthrow the Nationalist government. Security police captured Mandela and other MK leaders. After their trial in 1964 the judge sentenced them to life imprisonment.

Source B Key developments 1955–64

1955	A group of white women formed an organisation called 'The Black Sash' to oppose the removal of voting rights for coloureds and give practical help such as legal advice to blacks living in towns
1956	Women organised a mass demonstration against the Pass Laws
1956–61	Treason Trial Peasant revolts in rural areas
1957	Alexandra bus boycott
1959	Women protest at restrictions on making a living from brewing beer in Cato Manor (Durban)
1960	Sharpeville shooting followed by State of Emergency and banning of ANC, Communist Party and PAC.
1961	South Africa left the Commonwealth to become a Republic.
1961	First acts of sabotage by Umkhonto we Sizwe against electric power stations and government offices in Johannesburg, Port Elizabeth and Durban.

Question

1 How far do you trust the historian who wrote Source **A**? Why?

2 Of what value is Source **A** to historians studying the history of apartheid?

Was it treason?

▶ ## Why did the treason trial become an embarrassment to the government?

Dawn, 5 December 1956. The security police arrested 156 men and women on the charge of High Treason – a crime which carried the death penalty (Source **A**). The accused all supported the Freedom Charter (see pages 38–9). The Nationalist Government wanted to prove they were communists guilty of planning a violent revolution. The trial lasted from 1956 to 1961. Between court appearances the accused were released on bail so that those who had not lost their jobs could continue to work for their living. However, 'banning orders' restricted them to areas near their homes and prevented them from attending political meetings.

For most of the time the trial was extremely boring. The Government's lawyers did not prepare their case well. So-called experts like, Professor Andrew Murray, from the University of Cape Town, gave evidence that the ideas of the Freedom Charter were communist. However, when tested on another document he thought it was communist without recognising that he had written it himself!

The government underestimated the skills of the accused. Joe Slovo, the communist white lawyer, conducted his own defence and cross-examined a Special Branch Detective, Jeremiah Mollson, who had just given evidence against the ANC.

Source B   From records of the treason trial, 1957

Slovo: Do you understand English?
Mollson: Not so well.
Slovo: Do you mean to say that you reported these speeches in English but you don't understand English well?
Mollson: Yes, Your Worship.
Slovo: Do you agree that your notes are a lot of rubbish?
Mollson: I don't know.

The trial became an embarrassment to the Government who had to withdraw charges against 65 of the accused, including the ANC President, Albert Lutuli. As the trial continued it attracted good publicity for the Freedom Charter and drew attention to the political skills of Nelson Mandela.

Source A   Picture of those accused of treason in 1956

Source C   Nelson Mandela, speaking at the treason trial, August 1960

We are not anti-white, we are against white supremacy . . . The Congress has consistently preached a policy of race harmony and we have condemned racialism no matter by whom it is professed.

In March 1961 the remaining 91 accused were found 'not guilty' of High Treason and set free.

Questions

1 Study Source **A** carefully. Why and how do you think this picture was made?

2 Who do you think gained most from the Treason Trial and why: the government or the Freedom Charter Movement?

Women demonstrate against the Pass Laws

In what way was this protest a triumph?

From 1952 the government decided that women as well as men had to carry passes. This would mean that if caught without a pass they too could be arrested, taken from their children without warning, and sent away from the towns. Women joined together in a campaign against the Pass Laws.

On 9 August 1956 26,000 women arrived outside the Union Buildings in Pretoria to deliver their protest to the new Prime Minister, Johannes Strijdom.

Source A   One of the leaders of these women, Helen Joseph, a white social worker and trade unionist, kept a journal, which later was smuggled from South Africa

Once or twice I turned around, and I could see only the faces of women, thousands and thousands of faces, following us . . .
'Strijdom, you have struck a rock!' they sang. 'You have touched the women!' Once again I saw that sea of faces that was only one face, the face of the people of South Africa. Faces in a shifting mass of colour, the green of the blouses, gold and pastel colour of Indian saris, bright reds and blues of head-scarves, whiteness of faces, blackness of faces, here and there a splash of coloured sunshade . . .

From, Helen Joseph, *Tomorrow's Sun*, 1966

The Prime Minister chose not to meet them.

Source B   During the protest, another of the women's leaders, Lilian Ngoyi, began to sing

. . . very softly at first, 'Nkosi Sikelele', 'God Bless Africa'. And then twenty thousand women joined her, until their voices rose to the very heavens. We sang with tears in our eyes, on our cheeks
. . . Then it was over. Down the terraces they came and into the streets, walking in quiet triumph to the bus ranks. For it was their triumph; it was the Prime Minister who had suffered defeat at their hands when he would not stay to face them.

***Tomorrow's Sun*, 1966**

Source C   The reunion of Lilian Ngoyi and Helen Joseph after 10 years of separation through banning by apartheid laws

The women's opposition slowed down the government but did not prevent it from making women carry passes. By 1959 the women's anti-pass campaign was over.

Questions

1 What provoked women to organise a campaign against the Pass Law?

2 Find evidence from Sources **A**, **B** and **C** that women of all races supported the demonstration.

3 What did the women's anti-pass campaign achieve?

50

Bus boycotts

What did the bus boycotts achieve?

Source A Alexandra, January 1957: people walking or cycling 15 kilometres to work in the city centre of Johannesburg instead of using the buses

Apartheid laws like the Group Areas Act (1950) and the Native Resettlement Act (1954) forced Africans, Coloureds and Indians to live in racially separate areas of towns and cities. One consequence was that now thousands of these people had longer distances to travel to work and used buses which made travel more expensive. The Government gave the bus companies money to help keep costs as low as possible. So when the bus companies tried to increase fares people protested by refusing to use them – a method of protest known as 'boycotting'.

Trouble caused by the boycotts

A bus boycott in the southern Transvaal township of Evaton in 1955 led to violent clashes between guards hired by the bus company and boycotters who tried to prevent others using the buses. Nine people died in the worst fighting in June 1956 and several houses were destroyed. One hundred police armed with sten guns restored order. When the bus company agreed to scrap the increase in fares the Evaton boycott ended. More bus boycotts followed (Source **A**). In Alexandra the Government tried to break the boycott.

Source B Albert Lutuli, President-General of the African National Congress 1952–67

> . . . The Pass weapon was used against walkers, taxis were held up for long periods while all drivers and passengers had their names taken, the cyclists were compelled to join walkers when the police deflated their tyres. The White Press went on talking about intimidation – by Africans.

From Albert Lutuli, *Let My People Go*, Fontana, 1962

However, the boycotters did not give up until their demands were met. Thousands of people discovered just how powerful they could be by uniting to take positive action.

---

1 Look at Source **A**.
   a) Give a reason why most people in this picture would have preferred to travel to and from work by bus.
   b) Explain why many refused to use the buses.

2 Look at Source **B**.
   a) What was the 'Pass weapon'?
   b) Why do you think the White Press talked about intimidation by Africans?

3 How reliable are Sources **A** and **B** as evidence?

4 What did those who opposed apartheid learn from the success of the bus boycotts?

Questions

Collaboration and resistance in the countryside

▶ Why was there conflict in the countryside?

Africans who did not have permits to work in towns had to live on the 'reserves' (see page 23). In 1951 the Bantu Authorities Act made local chiefs responsible for collecting taxes and putting government policies into action.

The government wanted to limit the number of cattle to reduce overcrowding on the reserves. In Witziehoek, northern Free State, people seized cattle before they could be slaughtered. They tore down fences to open up more land for grazing and fought with the police. When in 1957 Chief Abram Moilaw refused to force women to use 'Pass' books in Zeerust, Transvaal, the Government deposed him and banished him to another part of the country. The women destroyed their pass books. Murders, arrests, beatings, and more banishments followed (Source **C**).

The Sekhukhne chief, Kolane Kgoloko, was one of several chiefs who co-operated with the government. His people saw him as a 'collaborator' and killed him.

Then, in 1959, Dr Hendrik Verwoerd introduced his plan (see page 46) to turn the reserves into tribal homelands (Bantustans) where Africans could develop separately from whites. Some tribal leaders, including a nephew of Nelson Mandela in the Transkei, saw this as an opportunity to escape from white rule and restore the traditional power of the chiefs over their people. Most Africans, however, rejected the 'Bantustans'.

Source A   Nelson Mandela, in *Long Walk to Freedom*, 1994

There was no doubt that Daliwonga (KD Mantanzima) was collaborating with the government . . . There were reports that *impis* (traditional warriors) from Mantanzima's headquarters had burned down villages that opposed him. There were several assassination attempts against him.

Source B   Albert Lutuli, in *Let My People Go*, 1962

To us the Bantustan means the home of disease and miserable poverty, the place where we shall be swept into heaps in order to rot, the dumping ground of 'undesirable elements', delinquents, criminals created especially in the towns and cities by the system. And the place where old and sick people are sent when the cities have taken what they had to give by way of strength, youth, and labour . . . Our home is in the white man's garbage can . . . The land to which we have been allocated is sometimes just aloes and stones . . . The people are shabbily clad, animals are feeble and bony . . .

Source C   Huts ablaze at Weenen, Natal, after the police ordered residents to leave in 1958

*Q*uestio

1   Find three reasons for resistance in the countryside.

2   Why did some African chiefs collaborate and others resist government policies?

The banished people

► **What happened to those banished from the homelands for resisting the Government?**

In 1962 Helen Joseph (see page 50) risked punishment herself by touring the country to find out (Source **A**).

Source A Map showing the route of Helen Joseph's journeys to visit the banished people

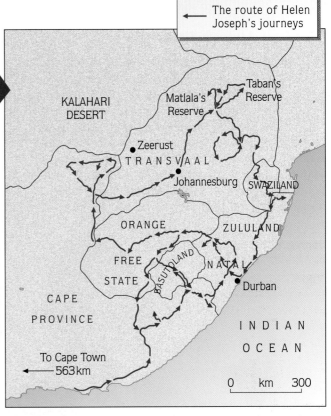

The route of Helen Joseph's journeys

Source B Abraham Mogale was one of many banished from Zeerust in 1958:

Before departing from Zeerust I was given an allowance of two pounds . . . I am not in employment; . . . I have been banished to the remotest part of Northern Zululand on the boundary of Swaziland. There is no transport facility in this place . . . The nearest hospital and doctor is thirty-nine miles from where I am . . . Life is not worth living.

Quoted in Helen Joseph, *Tomorrow's Sun*

Source C The Government banished Chief Miya from Natal to work on a farm in the Transvaal, where he had

to live in a hut which was so broken that the rain came in and made everything wet.

Source D The Seopa family, a mother and five children, banished from the Matlala Reserve in the Northern Transvaal to the Tabans reserve about a hundred miles away

We were brought to this place in a police van, We reached here in the late afternoon. My youngest child was then five years old. For myself and my five children there was then only one small hut . . . There was nothing at all in the hut for us, and we had only what we had brought for ourselves, but nothing to dig in the ground.

Mrs Seopa, quoted in Helen Joseph, *Tomorrow's Sun*

Source E One poor woman described the difficulty she had to persuade the authorities to bring home for burial the body of her banished husband.

They brought him on a Sunday and we buried him. But his body was in the coffin with only a shirt and trousers, not even shoes on his feet. And they did not bring any of his things

Mngabo Ranoto, quoted in Helen Joseph, *Tomorrow's Sun*

Questions

1 **a)** Use the evidence in Sources **A** to **E** to describe what it was like to be banished.
    b) What do these sources suggest about the kind of person Helen Joseph was?

2 Why do you think Helen Joseph smuggled her journal out of South Africa?

Sharpeville!

▶ ## Who was responsible for the Sharpeville massacre?

The Pan African Congress

ANC leaders like Albert Lutuli believed it essential to demonstrate multi-racial unity at a time when the government argued that separation of the races was natural and what everyone wanted. However, not all Africans in the ANC wanted the ANC to be a multi-racial organisation. They worried that whites and Indians had gained too much influence in the ANC and that some of them were communists. Robert Sobukwe (Source **A**) was a lecturer in African languages at the University of Witwatersrand.

Source A Robert Sobukwe, the first President of the PAC

Source B Sobukwe wanted the following

Government of the Africans by the Africans, and for the Africans, with everybody who owes his only loyalty to Africa and is prepared to accept the democratic rule of the African majority being regarded as African.

In 1959 Sobukwe and others broke away from the ANC to form the rival Pan African Congress. The PAC found support among frustrated young people in townships like Sharpeville.

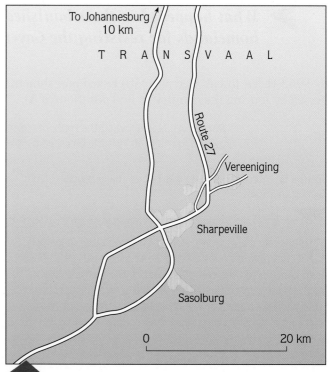

Source C Sharpeville

Sharpeville, 21 March 1960

By the standards of the time Sharpeville was a model township with neat rows of houses with running water, sanitation, street lighting and even weekly film shows. It was built to provide new homes for people living in an overcrowded and disease-ridden part of Vereeniging, a steel manufacturing centre fifty miles south of Johannesburg (Source **C**). The people who volunteered to move there gave little suppport to organisations like the ANC. However, by 1959, young people who had grown up in Sharpeville had difficulty finding jobs because the big factories preferred to employ 11,000 migrant workers from the reserves.

To win the support of young Africans in townships like Sharpeville, the PAC tried to upstage the ANC by organising a rival anti-pass campaign. The plan was to refuse to carry passes and to demonstrate peacefully outside police stations to demand arrest.

On 21 March 1960, a crowd of 5000 arrived outside the wire fence surrounding the Sharpeville police station. There was a tussle when those at the front trampled part of the fence and a police officer fell. Onlookers in the crowd pushed forward to see what was happening.

Source D Humphrey Tyler, *Drum* magazine, 1960

Then the shooting started. We heard the chatter of a machine gun, then another, then another. There were hundreds of women, some of them laughing. They must have thought the police were firing blanks. One woman was hit about ten yards from our car. Her companion, a young man, went back when she fell. He thought she had stumbled. He looked at the blood on his hands and said: 'My God, she's gone!'

Hundreds of kids were running, too. One little boy had on an old blanket coat, which he held up behind his head, thinking perhaps, that it might save him from the bullets . . .

Before the shooting I heard no warning to the crowd to disperse. There was no warning volley . . .

The police have claimed they were in desperate danger because the crowd was stoning them . . . The police have also said that the crowd was armed with 'ferocious weapons' which littered the compound after they fled . . . I saw no weapons, although I looked carefully, and afterwards studied the photographs of the death scene.

The police killed sixty-nine people – many shot in the back. Some 180 people were wounded. More people died in another demonstration at Langa township near Cape Town. All eyes were on South Africa. Governments and people all round the world expressed shock and horror at the action of the South African police. Huge crowds attended the funerals of the victims. Albert Lutuli, the ANC President, publicly burnt his pass book to show his sympathy with those killed at Sharpeville and Langa. He called for a nationwide stay-at-home protest. There was widespread support. Police and troops had to force Africans out of the townships to go to work. Businesses and trade suffered. The Prime Minister, Dr Verwoerd, declared a State of Emergency and banned both the ANC and PAC. The police arrested 18,000 people, including Albert Lutuli.

Questions

1   Does Source **B** show any real difference between the views of the ANC and PAC? Explain your answer (see page 39).

2   Why was the PAC formed?

3   In what ways were each of the following responsible for the Sharpeville shootings: the PAC; the police; the employment of migrant workers; apartheid?

4   **a)**   What evidence is there in Source **D** that the demonstrators were taken unawares when the shooting started?
   b)   Does Source **E** prove that Source **D** is reliable evidence? Explain your answer.

Source E   The scene after the Sharpeville shooting

The consequences of the Sharpeville shootings

 ### Were Nelson Mandela and the others freedom fighters or outlaws?

The Sharpeville shootings provoked a violent response. On 16 December 1961 Umkhonto we Sizwe (Spear of the Nation or MK for short, page 48) launched a campaign of bombing and sabotage on power stations and government buildings (Source **A**).

Source B   MK leaflet

Source A   An act of sabotage

The people's patience is not endless. The time comes in the life of any nation when there remains only two choices: submit or fight. That time has now come to South Africa. We shall not submit and we have no choice but to hit back by all means in our power in defence of our people, our future and our freedom . . .

The commander-in-chief of this guerilla army was Nelson Mandela. His High Command included Walter Sisulu and Joe Slovo, a white communist who helped forge links with the Soviet Union to obtain weapons and explosives. MK was careful to remain 'separate' from the ANC, whose leader, Albert Lutuli, received the Nobel Peace Prize four days before their first bombs exploded. They chose targets which would cause a minimum loss of life. However, Poqo, the newly formed military wing of the PAC, and another, mainly white, terrorist organisation called the African Resistance Committee (ARC) deliberately chose civilian targets to create maximum terror. Young Africans began to leave South Africa secretly to train in guerilla warfare in independent African countries, and in the Soviet Union and China.

'On the run'

From now on Mandela was an outlaw, 'on the run', staying for a short while in different houses, adopting the different disguises of a gardener or a chauffeur. It was a hard and lonely time not just for him but his wife, Winnie, and family, who saw very little of him. During the day he slept and then studied the guerilla tactics of Boer generals during the war and read the works of famous revolutionaries; at night he went to work as a 'Freedom Fighter'. In 1962 he toured Africa and visited Britain, making contacts and building support. But Mandela was no match for BOSS, the sinister Bureau of State Security, who were waiting for him on his return to South Africa.

Source C   From Fatima Meer, *Higher Than Hope*, 1988

Winnie was at work where somebody showed her the paper. She read the headlines: POLICE SWOOP ENDS TWO YEARS ON THE RUN, and under that, NELSON MANDELA IS UNDER ARREST. She swayed but a friend caught hold of her and she steadied herself . . . 'What now?' she wondered. She did not realise that she had effectively lost her husband, that her daughters would grow into women and bear their own children, and Nelson would still remain in prison.

At his trial the judge sentenced Mandela to only five years in prison but he was soon in court again on 9 October 1963. A raid on a farmhouse at Rivonia to the north of Johannesburg had uncovered the headquarters of MK and led to the discovery of incriminating documents. Among those arrested by the police were Walter Sisulu, Govan Mbeki, Elias Motsoaledi, Ahmed Kathrada, Raymond Mhlaba, Rusty Bernstein, Dennis Goldberg and Andrew Mlangeni. With Mandela they were on trial for their lives.

On 20 April their lawyer, Bram Fischer, asked Mandela to make an opening statement for the defence. It took Mandela four hours to read what was a devastating criticism of apartheid. He proudly admitted his part in fighting against it and for a democratic and free society.

Source D From Mandela's statement in April, 1964

Africans want to be allowed to own land in places where they work . . . African men want to have their wives and children to live with them where they work . . . Africans want to be allowed out after 11 o'clock at night and not to be confined to their rooms like little children, Africans want to be allowed to travel in their own country . . . Above all we want equal political rights. It is a struggle of the African people . . . a struggle for the right to live.

Mandela fully expected the death penalty, but his speech and world interest in the trial probably saved their lives. Rusty Bernstein was released because the evidence against him was weak, but was promptly re-arrested for being a communist. The judge sentenced the remaining eight to prison for life. The prisoners looked at each other and smiled. Mandela gave the thumbs up ANC salute. Dennis Goldberg shouted to his mother, 'Life! Life is wonderful!' Outside the crowd shouted 'Amandla!' ['power to the people'] and sang 'Nkosi Sikeleli' iAfrika'.

Source F *The Times* newspaper, June 1964

The verdict of history will be that the ultimate guilty party is the government in power – and that is the verdict of world opinion.

Questions

1 In what sense were the Sharpeville shootings in March 1960 a 'turning point' in South African history?

2 How did the tactics of MK differ from Poqo and the ARC?

3 How did Mandela's decision to become a freedom fighter affect his family life (Sources **C** and **E**)?

4 Explain *The Times* newspaper's comment on the South African government (Source **F**).

Source E The *Cape Argus*, 12 June 1964

MRS. WINNIE MANDELA, *wife of Nelson Mandela, leads her mother-in-law out of the crush after the verdict as the crowd shouts slogans and marches up and down.*

MRS. BERNSTEIN AND DAUGHTER IN TEARS

8 South Africa and the outside world

'A museum piece in our time ...' (Albert Lutuli)

 ### How was racism discredited?

In 1900 it was common for white people to believe that the white races were superior and that it was their duty to 'civilise' people who had a different coloured skin. Source **A** is a painting of Queen Victoria presenting a Bible to an African prince in 1861. What attitude does it suggest towards the Prince?

Source A Queen Victoria presenting a Bible at Windsor Castle

Lord Milner expressed the same attitude in a famous speech in Johannesburg on 18 May 1903.

Source B Lord Milner's speech

> . . . the white man should rule . . . The white man must rule because he is elevated by many steps above the black man; steps which it will take the black man centuries to climb.
>
> **From Cecil Headlam (ed.), *The Milner Papers*, 1931**

White people even looked for scientific proof to support their racist beliefs. They used the ideas of Charles Darwin in *The Origin of Species*, published in 1859, to

Source C A mass grave of Jews at Nordhausen concentration camp, Germany, 13 April 1945

claim that the white races were higher on the ladder of evolution than black people. They even tried to measure brain size and compare the shape of the head, colour of eyes and hair to classify people into racial groups. In Europe in the 1930s and 1940s Hitler and the Nazis took their racist beliefs to horrific extremes (Source **C**). Faced with Nazi race policies it became difficult for Europeans to claim that white people had a superior civilisation. Meanwhile, in South Africa a number of Afrikaners who were to become leaders, like Dr Verwoerd and B. J. Vorster, openly sympathised with the Nazis.

The Second World War soon became a fight to end the evil of racism. In August 1941 the British Prime Minister, Winston Churchill, and the American President, Roosevelt, signed the Atlantic Charter – sixteen other countries signed it too. It set out their war aims: to ensure freedom in the world and to enable people to live without fear and want.

Source D   The Atlantic Charter also stated its aim

. . . to respect the right of all people to choose the form of government under which they will live.

Did this mean that black people would be free at the end of the war? In August 1943 the committee of the All Africa Convention, which represented both Africans and Indians, made a declaration.

Source E   The All Africa Convention's declaration

The war is nearing its end . . . Still, this does not mean that Hitlerism, the creed of racial superiority is defeated. The white rulers of South Africa, with views so similar to Hitler's race theories, will not voluntarily give us our freedom and our rights.

The ANC Youth League, formed in 1943, took much of its inspiration from the words of Anton Lembede.

Source F   Anton Lembede's speech at an ANC Conference

Look at my skin, it is black, black like the soil of Mother Africa. We must verily [truly] believe that we are inferior to no other race on earth . . . We must develop race pride.

The ANC appointed a special committee to interpret the Atlantic Charter from the African point of view. In 1945 they published a booklet, 'Africans' Claims'.

Source G   From 'Africans' Claims'

We demand the abolition of discrimination based on race . . . and the extension to all adults regardless of race of the right to vote and be elected to Parliament . . .

Quoted in G. Mbeki, *The Struggle for Liberation*, Cape Town, 1992

South Africa's leader, General Smuts played an important part in creating the United Nations Organization which in 1948 issued a Declaration of Human Rights setting out people's hopes for a better world. Racism was officially dead. There was only one race – the human race. However, 'unofficially' racism was still very much alive. It puzzled people that General Smuts was in no hurry to put an end to racism in South Africa. When the ANC President reminded the government of the service non-whites had given during the war there was no response. While racism was discredited in the rest of the world South Africa became the only country to set up a system of laws which discriminated on the basis of race.

Questions

1   How has the artist of Source **A** made Queen Victoria look superior?

2   Using Sources **A** and **B** explain how white people in Milner's time thought they could help black people become civilised?

3   Explain how the behaviour of Nazi Germany (Source **C**) helped to turn people against racism.

4   Look at Sources **E**, **F** and **G**. To what extent did the Second World War help Africans in their struggle against white racism?

South Africa and world opinion

What changes were taking place?

In 1948 when the National Party came to power most of Africa was ruled by white people as part of their European Empires. By 1968 a massive change had taken place. Most African countries had become independent.

Source A   Africa in 1968

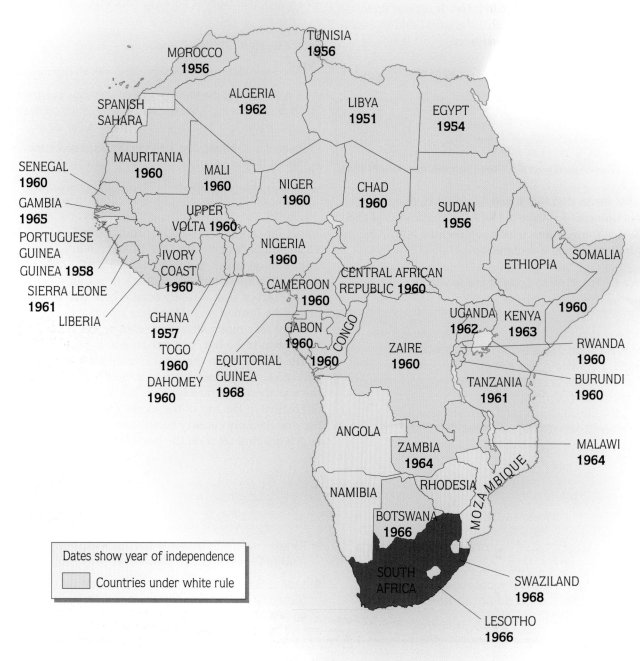

Harold Macmillan, the British Prime Minister, warned South Africans about this revolution when he addressed the Parliament in Cape Town on 3 February 1960.

Source B Harold Macmillan, *Pointing the Way*, 1972

> . . . the most striking of all the impressions I have formed since I left London a month ago is the strength of this African national consciousness. The wind of change is blowing through this continent . . . We must accept it as a fact . . .

The reaction of the South African government led by Dr Verwoerd, was to resist 'the wind of change' by trying to make sure that countries next to them had 'friendly' governments. They sent help to the Portuguese government in Angola and Mozambique against African rebels who were fighting for freedom and independence. The ANC secretly became their allies. The government sent help to Ian Smith when he declared independence for the white minority ruling Rhodesia in 1965. The following year they refused to obey United Nations orders to give up control of South West Africa for which they had been given a temporary responsibility at the end of the Second World War. SWAPO (South West African People's Organisation) freedom fighters became increasingly active there.

Meanwhile in the rest of Africa new countries were determined to end the evil of apartheid. The Organisation of African Unity, formed in 1963, made liberation of the people of South Africa its top priority. Around the world attitudes towards apartheid hardened, leaving the white government of South Africa increasingly isolated.

Key Events	
1952	The United Nations condemned apartheid
1962	The United Nations recommended economic sanctions against South Africa
1963	Olympic Games committee refused to accept racially segregated teams
1970	Cricket tour of the United Kingdom cancelled
1971	A boycott in the United Kingdom of banks lending money to South Africa
1973	Organisation of Petroleum Exporting Countries (OPEC) banned oil sales to South Africa
1974	South Africa banned from membership of the United Nations

In countries around the world groups formed to organise boycotts of South African products and protests to disrupt sports fixtures (Sources **C**, **D** and **E**).

Source C Extracts from a Bristol Anti-Apartheid Scrapbook in the 1960s

Demonstration

Bristol Anti-Apartheid Group will demonstrate in Broadmead tomorrow and next Saturday to call attention to Dr Verwoerd's treatment of political prisoners.

BARCLAYS BANK HAS BOUGHT £6000,000 OF SOUTH AFRICAN GOVT. DEFENCE BONDS

PICKET THIS THURSDAY 1.10

JAN 20TH

Queens Road branch next to Debenham's

Springboks!

WHY
NO
BLACK
TEAM
MEMBERS?

Bristol Anti-Apartheid

invites you to an interdenominational meeting, to hear

Bishop Trevor Huddleston speak on

THE IMMORALITY OF APARTHEID

LEAFLETS HAND-OUT AT DOCKS

Four members of Bristol branch of the Anti-Apartheid movement distributed 800 leaflets to dockers at the entrance to Avonmouth Docks today.

They urged a boycott on trade with South Africa.

Five thousand leaflets have been printed and follow-up campaigns are planned at the factories of Bristol Aeroplane Co. and Bristol Siddeley Engines.

MEET

HORFIELD COMMON

1.30 SATURDAY DEC 31

TO TELL THE SPRINGBOKS TO GO HOME AND BRING BACK THEIR AFRICAN BROTHERS

MARCH TO GROUND

Anti-apartheid

A public meeting to form an anti-apartheid group in Bristol will be held on Thursday at 7.30 p.m. in the Friends Meeting House, River Street, St Jude's.

Source D Boycott badges worn in Bristol by Anti-Apartheid campaigners

The African National Congress welcomed boycotts which were one form of sanction (an economic measure taken to persuade a country to follow a certain course of action) that any individual could take part in.

Source F Albert Lutuli, in *Let My People Go*, 1962

The economic boycott of South Africa will entail undoubted hardship for Africans. We do not doubt that. But if it is a method which shortens the day of bloodshed, the suffering for us will be a price we are willing to pay.

Sanctions

Governments were not always so happy about sanctions. Britain, France and the United States had huge investments in South Africa. They feared that sanctions would harm not only their businesses but also cause hardship for those who worked for them. Also this was the time of the Cold War between the Western Powers and the Soviet Union. Some governments chose to believe the propaganda of the South African government that a black government would lead to a communist take-over and that all the mineral wealth of the country would fall into the hands of the Soviet Union (Source **G**).

Source E One campaigner recalls the protest against the South African Rugby Tour of Britain in 1969

One part of the protest action was centred on the Bristol Hotel where they stayed the night before the match. The Hotel itself was picketed [a group of people tried to persuade people not to enter the hotel] on the outside, whilst selected demonstrators booked meals in the restaurant and let off stink-bombs in there and other parts of the Hotel. Two of our members from London had booked a room for the night and, on the internal phones, spent most of the night ringing the rooms on the floor which had been booked for the tourists. Also, the fire alarms were set off and the Hotel evacuated twice.

As for the match itself – there was a picket of the ground whilst two efforts to disrupt the match were planned. One which involved specially made smoke bombs had to be abandoned at the last moment when it was learnt that the police had been informed. The second involved a small group of ticket holders with match boxes full of tin-tacks, trying to scatter them on the pitch at half-time. . . . The match was held up whilst players and officials attempted to clear the pitch.

From Jack Evans, *Thirty Years of Campaigning*, 1994

Source G South Africa's share of the world's mineral wealth

Mineral	% World reserves in South Africa	Use
Gold	51	World's money
Platinum	83	Car exhausts, jewellery
Chromite	81	Steel
Manganese	78	Metals
Diamonds	50	Gems and industry
Uranium	25	Nuclear power
Vanadium	49	Steel
Titanium	15	Aircraft engines
Asbestos	14	Cement
Fluorspar	35	Steel
Vermiculite	40	Insulation

South Africa White Paper on Defence, 1977

There was another fear to do with the Cold War. If the Cape fell into Russian hands it could affect vital oil supplies to the West (Source **H**). For this reason Western leaders claimed that South Africa was needed in the fight against Communism and must be sent weapons to protect the sea route round the Cape. South Africa was a vital part of the defence of the West and this was more important than trying to change apartheid. As the wealthiest, fastest growing, most powerful state in Africa, the West must make sure South Africa was on its side.

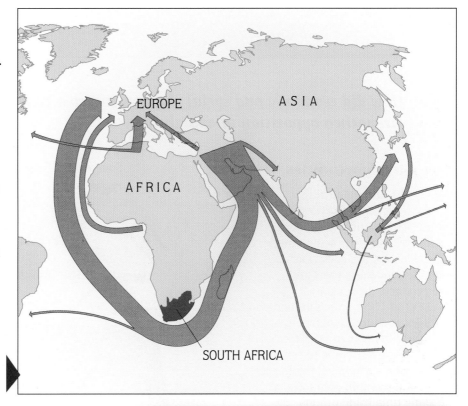

Source H Main oil routes, 1973

Some Western observers claimed that the South African government was judged too harshly.

Source I From L. Gann and P. Duignam, *South Africa, War, Revolution or Peace?* 1978

Few countries have acquired greater unpopularity during the last three decades than South Africa . . . South Africa is condemned for what is often overlooked elsewhere . . . on any scale that ranks the 'badness' of regimes South Africa would not rank at the top or even near the top . . . almost all communist states oppress and exploit their people more than does South Africa . . . as many as 80 million people have died in Soviet labour camps and prisons since 1917 but we seek to work towards good relations with Russia . . . Why is South Africa so different? Even in the African continent, South Africa cannot be given the 'highest marks' for oppression and exploitation. The claims for the title are numerous – Uganda, Ethiopa, Sudan, Burundi, Guinea, Angola, Mozambique . . . To date, no UN or OAU resolution has condemned any of these states.

However, many anti-apartheid campaigners believed that apartheid was a fertile soil for developing communism. The longer apartheid lasted, the more its victims might turn to Russia for help (Source **J**).

Source J Sowing the seeds of communism

Questions

1 Which countries still under white rule in 1968 enabled South Africa to feel 'safe' (Source **A**)?

2 Using Sources **C**, **D** and **E** describe the methods people used to oppose apartheid.

3 Do you agree that Sources **G**, **H** and **I** prove why Western powers supported the South African government? Give your reasons.

4 Using the cartoon in Source **J** explain the reasons why the cartoonist thinks victims of apartheid might turn to the Soviet Union for help.

9 The road to freedom: 1964–82

Overview: economic and social changes

▶ **How did economic and social changes increase and strengthen opposition to apartheid?**

New job opportunities

From 1944 manufacturing became a bigger employer than mining. The number of workers needed for industries which made things like clothes, cars, washing machines, machine tools and food products grew from 855,000 in 1951 to 1.6 million by 1976. A shortage of labour increased job opportunities for blacks. Employers came to rely on black workers who filled the lower skilled and less well paid jobs. At the same time trade unions organized workers to protect their new jobs and to fight to improve wages and working conditions. From 1973 an increase in world oil prices led to a sharp rise in the cost of living and demands for higher wages. Between 1973 and 1976 over 200,000 black workers took part in strikes.

Rising standards of living for whites

A song written in 1962 (Source **A**) made fun of the changing lifestyle of those Afrikaners who once saw themselves as the 'Poor Whites'. The song is about a spoilt Afrikaner boy pestering his father to take him and his friends out in the large new family car, a Chevrolet. First he wants to be taken to an open air cinema called a 'Drive in', then to a fun-fair, then to a wrestling match, and then to a beach holiday in Durban. The chorus is a list of his favourite sweets and drinks.

Owning a car was only one sign of new wealth. A higher standard of living for whites meant owning a home with African servants, a large garden with a

Source A Song by Jeremy Taylor, 1962

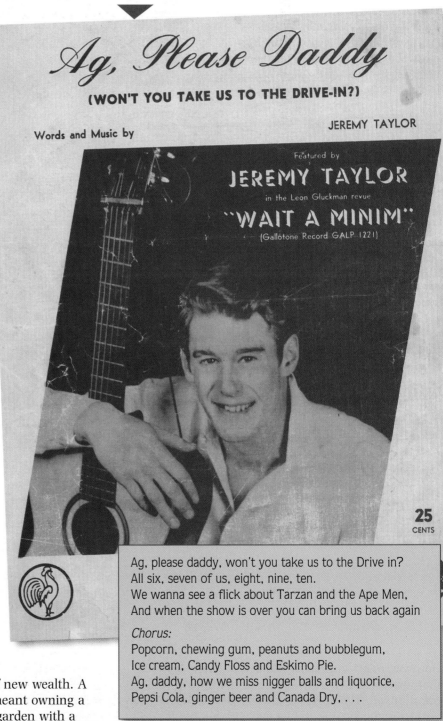

Ag, please daddy, won't you take us to the Drive in?
All six, seven of us, eight, nine, ten.
We wanna see a flick about Tarzan and the Ape Men,
And when the show is over you can bring us back again

Chorus:
Popcorn, chewing gum, peanuts and bubblegum,
Ice cream, Candy Floss and Eskimo Pie.
Ag, daddy, how we miss nigger balls and liquorice,
Pepsi Cola, ginger beer and Canada Dry, . . .

swimming pool, barbecues and getting a good suntan for most of the year.

Though better educated, the younger generation of whites grew up separated from blacks. Censorship and government control of the radio kept many whites ignorant of what life was really like for black people. The government did not allow television in South Africa until 1976.

Rising standard of living for blacks . . .

The standard of living for blacks improved too, though for most it remained a long way below those of whites. For black people, owning a car was also a sign of wealth and status. They developed similar tastes to white people for clothes, furniture, cosmetics, sweets, cigarettes, pop music and sport. However, apartheid kept the growing prosperity around them beyond their reach, adding to their frustration. Nevertheless, there was a small but growing black middle class. In Cape Town and Durban black people jokingly began to refer to this new black middle class as the 'ooscuse-me'. They included traders, businessmen, clerks, civil servants, teachers and nurses who had the education and skill to organize opposition to apartheid.

Population changes

In the 1960s the population rapidly increased. However, African families chose to have more babies than white families (Source **B**). As a result, by 1985, the African population was younger than the white population: 46.5 per cent of Africans were under 15, compared with 26.5 per cent of whites. Black school children took a leading part in a new rebellion against apartheid.

Urbanization

More jobs in industries attracted more people to live in towns and led to the creation of new towns close to industrial centres. Meanwhile, to please white farmers, between 1967 and 1982 the government forced nearly two million African farmers to move from land outside the homelands to live inside homelands where there was no farm land left to give them. By 1980 over 50 per cent of Africans in South Africa lived in the homelands. In many of the homeland townships houses did not have electricity or running water and there were no local shopping centres, cinemas or parks. Millions had to travel long distances to work every day which could take several hours.

Source C Changes in the percentage of the population living in towns:

	All	White	Coloured	Asian	African
1960	47	84	68	83	32
1970	48	87	74	87	33
1980	54	88	75	91	49

From W. Beinart, *Twentieth-Century South Africa*, 1994

Source B The growth of the population in South Africa

Year	Total population	% white	% coloured	% Asian	% African
1951	12,671,452	20.9	8.7	2.9	67.5
1970	21,794,328	17.3	9.4	2.9	70.4
1991	38,268,720	13.2	8.6	2.6	75.6

From W. Beinart, *Twentieth-Century South Africa*, 1994

Questions

1 Study Source **A**.
   a) What kind of lifestyle could Afrikaner children expect in 1962?
   b) How would Afrikaner parents have compared their own childhood with that of their children in 1962?

2 Suggest how each of the following created conditions to strengthen opposition to apartheid:
   • new job opportunities;
   • rising standards of living;
   • television;
   • population changes;
   • urbanization.

Freedom fighters and Black Consciousness

▶ **What happened to the ANC and PAC?**

The fate of the resistance

In 1960 the ANC sent its Deputy President, Oliver Tambo (Source **A**), abroad to set up an External Mission. He got out of South Africa just in time. By 1964 those leaders of the resistance who were not in exile, like Tambo, were in prison on Robben Island. The PAC too survived in exile but remained a bitter rival of the ANC. Resistance to apartheid from exile took two forms: guerilla warfare and diplomacy.

Source A Oliver Tambo

Guerilla warfare

Friendly countries provided bases for ANC and PAC guerillas (Source **B**). Three problems faced the guerillas: lack of training, poor equipment and the white allies of the South African government who ruled Angola, Rhodesia (Zimbabwe) and Mozambique. During 1967–8 ANC guerillas and Zimbabwean freedom fighters fought against Rhodesian forces and South African police but with little success. However, the collapse of white rule in Angola (1974), Mozambique (1975) and Zimbabwe (1979) gave them a better chance of causing trouble inside South Africa.

Source B Map showing where the ANC and PAC guerilla bases were

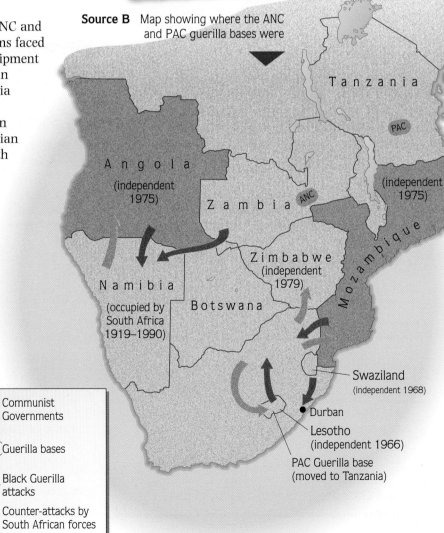

Diplomacy

Fierce and sometimes violent quarrels divided and weakened the PAC. Oliver Tambo, on the other hand, with the help of Joe Slovo, found allies in the United Nations from Africa, Scandinavia and communist countries which included the newly independent Mozambique and Angola. However, these links with communists caused the USA and other Western governments to treat the ANC with suspicion.

▨ Communist Governments

PAC ⬭ ANC ⬭ Guerilla bases

➡ Black Guerilla attacks

➡ Counter-attacks by South African forces

Steve Biko and Black Consciousness

The creation of separate universities for Africans after 1958 led to a big increase in African students. Many joined the National Union of South African Students (NUSAS) despite the fact that most of its members were English-speaking whites. The union was multi-racial and its leaders were often in trouble for opposing apartheid. However, in 1969 a black medical student at Natal University dismayed the white students by forming a separate all-black South African Students' Organization (SASO). His name was Steve Biko. He and his supporters helped set up the Black Communities Project to develop black self-help schemes. They further offended many white liberals in 1971 by forming a political organization called the Black People's Convention. Their aim was to promote the ideas of 'Black Consciousness'.

Source C   Barney Pityana, a SASO leader

This means that black people must build themselves into a position of nondependence upon whites . . .

Quoted in D. Woods, *Biko*, 1978

Biko deliberately used the term 'black' to mean all non-white South Africans. Writing under the name Frank Talk, he voiced his thoughts (Source **D**).

Source D   Frank Talk, 'I write what I like', *SASO Student Newspaper*

All in all the black man has become a shell, a shadow of a man, completely defeated, drowning in his own misery, a slave . . .
No wonder the African child learns to hate his heritage in his days at school. So negative is the image presented to him that he tends to find solace [comfort] only in close identification with white society . . . No doubt, therefore, part of the approach envisaged in bringing about 'Black Consciousness' has to be directed to the past, to seek to rewrite the history of the black man and to produce in it the heroes who form the core of the African background.

The University of Natal expelled Steve Biko in 1972 for 'inadequate academic performance'. 'The System', as he called the Government and police, saw him as a trouble maker and banned him in 1973 to King William's Town where he worked for the Black Community Programme. At first many whites believed that Steve Biko's ideas encouraged black racism – especially among young blacks. In 1977 the 'System' decided he had to be silenced, as described by white journalist, Donald Woods (Source **E**).

Source E   By Donald Woods

On Tuesday, September 6, 1977, a friend of mine named Stephen Biko was taken by South African political police to Room 619 of the Sanlam Building in Strand Street, Port Elizabeth, Cape Province, where he was handcuffed, put into leg irons, chained to a grille, and subjected to twenty-two hours of interrogation in the course of which he was tortured and beaten, sustaining several blows to the head that damaged his brain fatally, causing him to lapse into a coma and die six days later.

From D. Woods, *Biko*

The Police Minister, Kruger, said Biko had died from a hunger strike. Later an inquest decided that brain damage was the cause of death but that none of the Security Police was guilty of a criminal offence.

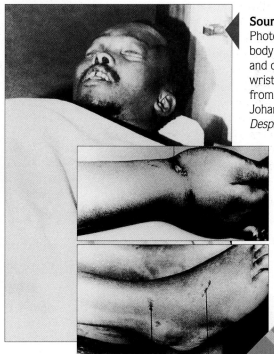

Source F
Photographs of the body of Steve Biko and of injuries to his wrist and ankles, from the Johannesburg *Daily Despatch*

Questions

1 What **a)** helped and **b)** hindered the ANC and PAC in their resistance to apartheid after 1964?

2 Explain the purpose of Black Consciousness.

3 Do you believe Steve Biko was murdered? If so, why?

The children of SOWETO

▶ ***Why did the children of SOWETO rebel?***

In SOuth WEstern TOwnship (SOWETO), which lies on the outskirts of Johannesburg, overcrowded secondary schools had class sizes of as high as 60 to 100 pupils. Lack of text books and a shortage of qualified teachers forced schools to teach in two shifts. In 1976 the Education Minister announced that half of all subjects (including maths, history and geography) had to be taught in Afrikaans. Steve Biko, when asked for evidence of Black Consciousness among the younger generation, had made his feelings clear (Source **A**).

In one word: Soweto!

Source A Steve Biko interviewed by Bernard Zylstra, July 1977

On 16 June SOWETO schools joined together in a mass demonstration (Source **B**).

Source B The SOWETO demonstration, 1976

Fifteen thousand youths, ranging in age from 10 to 20 years, were ready to march off, bearing slogans written on cardboard torn from packing cases or on the stiff covers of exercise books . . . the slogans were simple and to the point:
    Down with Afrikaans
    Afrikaans is oppressors' language
    Abolish Afrikaans
    Blacks are not dustbins – Afrikaans stinks.

From Alan Brooks and Jeremy Brickhill, *Whirlwind before the storm*, 1980

The police went into action (Sources **C** and **D** and Source **F** on page 5).

I was there among them, I saw what happened. The children picked up stones, they used dustbin lids as shields and marched towards the machine guns . . . the determination, the thirst for freedom in children's hearts, was such that they were prepared to face those machine guns with stones. That is what happens when you hunger for freedom, when you want to break those chains of oppression. Nothing else seems to matter.

From Winnie Mandela, *Part of My Soul*, 1984

Source C Winnie Mandela

Rioting, class boycotts, school burnings, attacks on police and government buildings followed and spread to other townships on the Rand and to Cape Town and the eastern Cape. By the end of the year 576 people had been killed and 2389 wounded.

Source D Casspir armoured personnel carriers move into Soweto

Questions

1 a) Why do you think the South African government wanted half of the subjects in black schools taught in Afrikaans?
b) Explain whether you think this was the main cause or just the 'trigger' for the children's protest?

2 Explain Steve Biko's claim that the Soweto protest was evidence of black consciousness among the younger generation (Source **A**)?

Chief Buthelezi and Inkatha

▶ ## Why did supporters of the ANC and PAC oppose Buthelezi?

In 1978 the PAC leader, Robert Sobukwe died of cancer. Among the guests invited by his family to the funeral in Graaf-Reinet was the Zulu leader, Chief Mangosuthu Gatsha Buthelezi (Source **A**). He had been to the University of Fort Hare with Robert Sobukwe. Both had been members of the ANC Youth Wing.

However, unlike Chief Albert Lutuli, the Zulu President of the ANC, Buthelezi cooperated with the government's creation of Bantustans in 1951. The government rewarded his cooperation by making him chief of the Buthelezi tribe in 1957 instead of his older brother, Mceleli. He became Chief Minister of the newly created homeland of KwaZulu in 1972. Nevertheless, Buthelezi rejected full independence for KwaZulu, opposed apartheid, and demanded the release of Nelson Mandela and other political prisoners. In March 1975 he set up a powerful political organization, called Inkatha ya KwaZulu. It aimed to replace apartheid with a non-

racist system of sharing power in South Africa which would allow the Zulu nation to be self-governing. In the process, Buthelezi made a number of enemies.

Source B Steve Biko on Buthelezi in an interview with Bernard Zylstra, July 1977

▼

We oppose Gatsha. He dilutes the cause by operating on a government platform.

The presence of Buthelezi at the funeral of Robert Sobukwe caused outrage (Source **C**).

Source C The Johannesburg *Sunday Post*, 12 March 1978

▼

Two hundred militants – aged from eight to eighteen – overran the coffin and wreaths in their effort to get at the man they brandished a sell out. . . . All pleas for peace were ignored as the youths spat in his face and some threw handfuls of silver at him, alluding to Judas Iscariot . . .

Eventually, Bishop Tutu succeeded in persuading Buthelezi to leave . . . accompanied by a rain of stones and a crescendo of jeering chants from the youths: 'Let Gatsha go like a dog . . . he is a boer and a bantu. He is not of Azania [the name for South Africa used by supporters of Black Consciousness].'

◀ **Source A** Chief Gatsha Buthelezi

Questions

1 Suggest why Buthelezi attended the funeral of Robert Sobukwe?

2 **a)** How do you explain the reaction of the youths to Buthelezi's presence at Sobukwe's funeral (Source **C**)?
b) Describe how you think Zulus would have reacted to the way the crowd treated Buthelezi.

Prisoner 466/64

▶ ### How did Nelson Mandela survive his years of imprisonment?

Source A Map of Robben Island

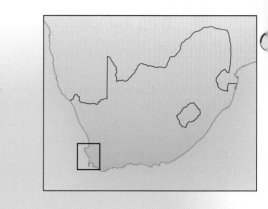

Robben Island is clearly visible from the centre of Cape Town only 7 miles off the coast.

Robben Island

CAPE TOWN

In May 1963 Nelson Mandela was sent to the maximum security prison on Robben Island to serve five years imprisonment with hard labour.

First impressions

Source B Nelson Mandela, in *Long Walk to Freedom*, 1994

The docks at Cape Town were swarming with armed police and nervous plain-clothes officials. We had to stand, still chained, in the hold of the old wooden ferry, which was difficult as the ship rocked in the swells off the coast. A small porthole above was the only source of light and air. The porthole served another purpose as well: the warders enjoyed urinating on us from above. It was still light when we were led on deck and saw the island for the first time. Green and beautiful, it looked at first more like a resort than a prison.

After a brief visit back to the mainland for the Rivonia trial Mandela returned to the island in June 1964 as prisoner 466/64 to begin a life sentence for High Treason.

Prison routine

For the next 18 years Mandela and his comrades spent their nights alone in damp cells on mats covered by three thin blankets to keep them warm. During the day there was hard labour crushing stones into gravel, or working in the lime quarry or, especially if newspaper photographers were present, sewing jerseys. No watches or timepieces were allowed. Bells and whistles signalled the change of activities. Each week resembled the one before. Mandela worried that if he lost a sense of time he might go mad and so one of the first things he did was to make a calendar on the wall of his cell.

Source C Mandela sewing clothes

The other prisoners looked to Mandela to act as their spokesperson and leader. Both the PAC and ANC kept their organizations going on Robben Island. Mandela and Walter Sisulu used this as an opportunity to try to end the bitter rivalry between the two organizations and other political groups.

Source D Neville Alexander, in *Robben Island: our University*, 1988

Something that Nelson and Walter taught me, personally, was the whole question of respecting other people for their point of view, even if you disagreed with it. In other words the importance of being able to disagree while you continue to respect that person.

Some of the prison warders were more humane than others. An exception was Van Rensburg who arrived on the island after the assassination of Verwoerd in 1966. He had a small swastika tattooed on his wrist and did his best to make the prisoners' lives as wretched as possible. A visit from the sympathetic South African MP, Helen Suzman, gave Mandela an opportunity to complain, with the result that Van Rensburg was transferred from the island.

The prisoners took advantage of opportunities to study for qualifications and to learn from each other while they were doing hard labour.

Source E Neville Alexander

The other important thing which I still think is one of the most amazing things, was the fact that . . . people could present actual lessons, even lectures, while they were swinging a pick or shovelling lime.

Rare visits from family were very stressful and lasted for about half an hour (Source **F**).

Source F Nelson Mandela, in *Long Walk to Freedom*, 1994

I could see immediately that Winnie was under tremendous strain . . . The banning and harassment of my wife greatly troubled me: I could not look after her and the children, and the state was making it difficult for her to look after herself. My powerlessness gnawed at me. . . . Winnie was not able to visit me for another two years.

The only newspapers prisoners read were ones stolen from the guards or carelessly thrown away. Letters were censored. Telegrams were rare and usually brought bad news, such as the death of Mandela's eldest son, Thembekile (killed in a road accident) in 1969. Permission to attend the funeral was refused. During terrible moments like this he depended on the support of his friend, Walter Sisulu (Source **G**).

Source G Nelson Mandela, in *Long Walk to Freedom*, 1994

. . . I do not have words to express the sorrow, or the loss I felt. It left a hole in my heart that can never be filled.

I returned to my cell and lay on my bed . . . Finally, Walter came to me and knelt beside my bed, and I handed him the telegram. He said nothing, but only held my hand. I do not know how long he remained with me.

In March 1988 Nelson Mandela was transferred from Robben Island to Pollsmoor prison in Cape Town.

Source H Nelson Mandela's cell on Robben Island

1 **a)** How were prisoners treated on Robben Island?
   b) Why do you think prisoners were treated in this way?

2 Describe what Mandela and others did to survive imprisonment on Robben Island.

10 The apartheid state under siege 1978–89

The seeds of change

▶ **What pressures led to the downfall of apartheid?**

An unlikely reformer: Balthazaar Johannes Vorster

B. J. Vorster – Key dates	
1915	born 13 December, Jamestown, Cape Province
1942	imprisoned for his role as a *Stormjaer* (stormtrooper) in the pro-German Ossewabrandweg
1953	entered Parliament
1961	Minister of Justice
1966	Prime Minister
1976	revolt in Soweto and other townships
1977	death of Steve Biko in 1977 after police beatings while in detention
1978	became President, but resigned as a result of the Muldergate scandal

Source A B. J. Vorster, Prime Minister 1966–78

The assassination of Prime Minister Verwoerd in 1966 brought to power Balthazaar Johannes Vorster (Source **A**). He had proved himself to be a tough and ruthless enforcer of apartheid. As Minister of Justice from 1961 it was he who introduced laws to imprison opponents of apartheid without trial and detain witnesses for up to six months. One of the first things Vorster did when he became Prime Minister was to create a secret police force, the Bureau of State Security (BOSS). Over the next ten years he enforced the policy of creating Bantustans with great enthusiasm. Lorry loads of Africans were taken from 'white areas' and dumped in so-called 'homelands' (see pages 45–6) some of which became self-governing after 1971.

The seeds of change

Yet during Vorster's years in power there were growing signs that apartheid had begun to work against the interests of those who gained most from it – whites who owned businesses. Changes in industry meant that employers wanted more permanent skilled workers who could be trained to use new technology. They could no longer depend on temporary migrant labourers. The removal of black workers to Bantustans caused a shortage of permanent labour. Employers began to find ways around apartheid laws to employ more black workers because there were not enough whites to fill the jobs. Blacks realized that this gave them power to bargain for better conditions and wages. Between 1973 and 1975, widespread strikes by illegal black trade unions demonstrated this power. Vorster responded by setting up two investigations, the Riekert and Wiehahn Commissions, to find solutions to the labour shortage and strikes. In 1979 they recommended scrapping the reservation of jobs for whites and legalising African trade unions.

Too little, too late . . .

By now the evil reputation of apartheid threatened to damage trading relations with other countries. Foreign businesses in South Africa (Source **B**) came under pressure to justify co-operating with apartheid.

Source C
The growth of the police and defence forces and of military spending

	1974	*1977*	*1981*
South African Police	59,000	72,000	77,000
South African Defence Force (including reserves)	269,000	367,500	515,000
Estimated total armed personnel at any time	90,000	150,000	255,000
Military spending (excluding police)	R707m	R1,940m	R3,000m

From *The Apartheid War Machine*, IDAF, April 1980 and *Focus on Political Repression*, July–August, 1981

At the same time, unrest inside South Africa and growing tensions across South Africa's borders led to a huge increase in the police and armed forces (Source **C**). To encourage recruitment from 1975 the South African Defence Force treated black and white soldiers of the same ranks as equals. It became compulsory for white soldiers to salute senior black officers.

The Muldergate scandal

A serious error of judgement made in 1973 led to Vorster's downfall and shook Afrikaner confidence in the National Party. Vorster approved of a plan, supported by his Minister of Information, Dr Connie Mulder, for a secret 'propaganda war' to improve the image of apartheid abroad and silence its critics at home in South Africa. It involved using 64 million rand (£40 million) on bribes, projects and dirty tricks (Source **D**).

Discovery of how this money was used caused a scandal similar to another in America, called the 'Watergate Affair', which had forced President Nixon to resign in 1974. Despite a landslide election victory in 1977 the scandal first forced Vorster to give up being Prime Minister, on the grounds of 'ill-health', and to take on the less demanding job of President. He was eventually forced to resign in disgrace in 1978.

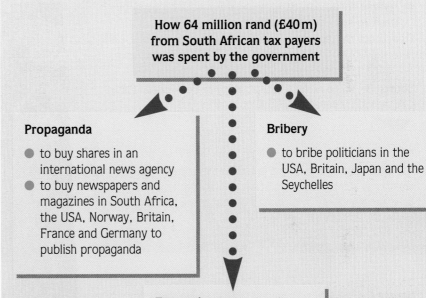

How 64 million rand (£40 m) from South African tax payers was spent by the government

Propaganda
- to buy shares in an international news agency
- to buy newspapers and magazines in South Africa, the USA, Norway, Britain, France and Germany to publish propaganda

Bribery
- to bribe politicians in the USA, Britain, Japan and the Seychelles

Entertainment
- to buy luxury properties in Miami, Cannes, London, Soweto and South Africa to entertain friends and clients of the South African government

Source D   The Muldergate scandal

Questions

1 What evidence is there that Vorster was responsible for some of the worst years of apartheid?

2 How did Vorster respond to growing pressures for change?

3 How does the secret propaganda war (Source **D**) by the Ministry of Information help explain why there was not greater international pressure against apartheid in the 1970s?

'Total strategy'

▶ Was 'total strategy' a failure?

The new leader of the National Party, P.W. Botha (Source **A**), developed a plan, called 'total strategy', to save the apartheid state (Source **E**). It aimed to:
● strengthen the alliance between the National Party, big business and the security forces which now ruled South Africa;
● reduce those causes of discontent which could be used to stir up a revolution;
● protect the apartheid state from enemies inside and outside South Africa.

Source B   Botha explains total strategy to the National Party congress in Durban, Natal, 15 August 1979

The world does not remain the same, and if we as a government want to act in the best interests of the country in a changing world, then we have to be prepared to adapt our policy to those things that make adjustment necessary, otherwise we die.

Source C   The Afrikaner journalist, Rian Malan, describing his father's reaction to Botha's reforms

He would sit in his armchair of an evening with a whiskey in hand and the day's newspapers spread out on his lap, drawing my attention to all that had changed or was about to change. President Botha had removed the ban on interracial love and marriage. President Botha had offered freedom to political prisoners who renounced violence. President Botha had promised 'just and peaceful' solutions to the country's problems. 'By the time Nelson Mandela gets out of jail,' said my father, 'there'll be nothing left for him to do . . . Like an American, my father thought that dismantling apartheid was mostly a question of allowing blacks to move to the front of the bus, use the drinking fountains, and sit alongside whites at lunch counters. He didn't grasp that the only issue was power.

Rian Malan, *My Traitor's Heart*, 1990

Source A   P.W. Botha

Source D   Nelson Mandela, in a letter smuggled from prison, gave his reaction

To see the real face of apartheid we must look beneath the veil of constitutional formulae, deceptive phrases and playing with words.
    The rattle of gunfire and the rumbling of Hippo armoured vehicles since June 1976 have once again torn aside the veil.

Nelson Mandela, letter published in 1980

Source E Total strategy in practice 1979–89

Policies	Reactions and consequences
To please big business, in 1979 Botha promised support for business interests and orderly reform. From 1979 businesses could employ blacks in certain skilled and semi-skilled jobs previously reserved for whites only.	This upset many white working class and lower middle class Afrikaners. In 1982 many left the National Party to join the newly formed Conservative Party led by Andries Treurnicht.
Relaxation of the Pass Laws (abolished completely in 1986) gave employers a larger permanent workforce so that they did not have to depend on temporary migrant workers.	The number of blacks living in towns rapidly increased.
African trade unions became legal (1979). It was hoped that this would improve relations with employers and create a more disciplined workforce.	Between 1979 and 1988 the number of blacks involved in strikes greatly increased: 1979 – 101 strikes (80% black workers) 1987 – 1000+ strikes (99% black workers)
To reduce causes of discontent more resources were put into education for blacks. Removal of many 'petty apartheid' restrictions – segregation no longer compulsory in hotels, restaurants and theatres in large cities.	The increase in the number of students at secondary school, college and university led to the formation, in 1979, of powerful youth organizations hostile to apartheid: COSAS (Congress of South African Students) and the Azanian Students Organization (AZASO).
1982, local residents of black townships could elect councillors with powers to raise money to govern townships by rents and taxes.	Many township blacks saw black councillors as 'collaborators' with apartheid.
1983–4 A new constitution allowed the election of white (178), Indian (45) and coloured (85) MPs to separate houses of the same parliament. It created a new office of State President, with wide ranging powers.	Blacks united in opposition to the new constitution.
To increase internal and external security the State Security Council (created in 1972) became more powerful. Under General Magnus Malan the leaders of the armed forces and Secret Police had a big influence on government decisions.	After the SOWETO revolt, 6000 young people from the townships left South Africa to train as ANC guerillas in Angola.

Questions

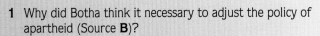

1 Why did Botha think it necessary to adjust the policy of apartheid (Source **B**)?

2 In what ways did Botha's 'total strategy' adapt or change apartheid (Source **E**)?

3 What evidence is there that the 'total strategy' did not have the consequences Botha intended (Source **E**)?

4 Compare Sources **C** and **D**.
a) In what ways was Nelson Mandela's reaction to 'total strategy' different from that of Rian Malan's father?
b) Why do you think their attitudes were different?

The armed struggle and external relations

▶ **Why did external threats to apartheid increase?**

New allies for the armed struggle

The independence of Angola and Mozambique from Portuguese rule in 1975, and Zimbabwe in 1980 brought Marxist governments to power. From Botha's point of view, South Africa now faced a serious threat of a united attack (a 'total onslaught') by its independent African neighbours backed by communist Russia (Source **A**). Angola provided a guerrilla training base for the ANC and a base from which the South West African People's Organization (SWAPO) could fight for Namibia's independence from South Africa. Support from Mozambique made it easier for the ANC to attack targets inside South Africa. Among the ANC's most spectacular attacks was a rocket attack in June 1980 on the Sasolberg refinery which made oil from coal, and in December 1982 a bomb explosion at the Koeberg nuclear power station.

Source A P. W. Botha saw communism as the biggest threat to the security of South Africa

There is no doubt in my mind that Russia is the dominating force in international affairs today . . . she wants to control the destiny of Africa, for its raw materials and the sea route round the Cape . . . the moment she succeeds . . . Russia will concentrate on isolating America from Europe.

P. W. Botha, then Minister of Defence, 1977

Source B Why neighbouring African states depended upon economic links with South Africa

How the South African government struck back

Despite their hatred of apartheid, neighbouring black states depended on economic links with South Africa (Source **B**). Botha's government tried to use this as a lever to force them not to

Map (Source B)

Railway link disrupted by civil war

ZAIRE

Port not efficiently run, causing bottlenecks

Dar-es-Salaam

Tanzam Railway

Benguela

Benguela Railway

ANGOLA

ZAMBIA

Cahora Bassa

MALAWI

Railway link disrupted by civil war

1983
40% of exports and 70% of imports routed through South Africa

SOUTH WEST AFRICA/NAMIBIA

1983
65–70% of foreign trade routed through South Africa

ZIMBABWE

BOTSWANA

Beira

MOZAMBIQUE

Hydro-electric power produced at Cahora Bassa fed to Maputo (Mozambique's capital) through the South African grid

1.5 million migrant miners from Malawi, Mozambique and Lesotho with families (3 million) dependent on them

SWAZI-LAND

Maputo

LESOTHO

Richards Bay

Durban

Cape Town

SOUTH AFRICA

East London

Port Elizabeth

0 km 1000

Modern efficiently-run ports

Source C South African soldiers leaving Angola

help the ANC and SWAPO. At the same time the South African secret service (BOSS) used methods such as parcel bombs to assassinate supporters of the guerillas living in exile, and gave support to anti-government forces in Angola and Mozambique. In 1984, South Africa bullied Mozambique into signing a 'non-aggression and good neighbourliness' pact called the Nkomati Accord. Nevertheless, two years later a false beacon on a South African hillside lured the Mozambique President Machel to death in a mysterious plane crash. Meanwhile, South Africa Defences forces pursued SWAPO guerrillas across the border of Namibia into Angola (Source **C**).

Sanctions and Archbishop Desmond Tutu

The United Nations ban on the sale of arms to South Africa in 1977 had little effect. South Africa developed its own weapons industry (ARMSCOR). With the help of Israel it became a nuclear power. However, the award of the Nobel Peace prize to an Anglican priest, Desmond Tutu (Source **D**), in 1984 gave international publicity to another non-violent but outspoken critic of apartheid.

Source D   Desmond Tutu

From 1985 the United States and EEC began to impose sanctions. This meant withdrawing business from South Africa. Sanctions prompted anxious white South African businessmen to travel to Zambia to meet ANC leaders.

Despite pressure from other Commonwealth leaders the British Prime Minister, Margaret Thatcher, opposed sanctions. However, she supported a visit to South Africa in 1986 by a group of 'Eminent Persons' from the Commonwealth to persuade the ANC and South African government to start talks. The South African

government forced the group to abandon their visit in anger after ordering air raids on what they claimed were ANC bases in the capitals of Botswana, Zambia and Zimbabwe – three countries who were members of the Commonwealth.

Source E   Margaret Thatcher still stated her opposition to sanctions, July 1986

> To me it is absolutely absurd that people should be prepared to put increasing power into the hands of the Soviet Union on the grounds that they disapprove of apartheid in South Africa.

Then the Anglican Church elected Desmond Tutu to become the first black Archbishop of Cape Town.

Source F   Desmond Tutu at a news conference in 1986

> I have no hope of real change from this government unless they are forced. We face a catastrophe in this land and only the action of the international community by applying pressure can save us . . . I call upon the international community to apply punitive sanctions against this government to help us establish a new South Africa – non-racial, democratic, participatory and just.

Tougher sanctions from America followed. By 1988, South Africa agreed to give Namibia its independence. Then, in 1989, the collapse of the Soviet Union removed Russia as a threat to the security of Southern Africa.

Questions

1 What do Sources **A** and **E** show that P. W. Botha and Margaret Thatcher had in common?

2 Use Source **B** to explain why economic links prevented a united attack on South Africa by its independent African neighbours?

3 What evidence is there that the independence of Angola and Zimbabwe helped SWAPO and the ANC?

4 Is is safe to conclude from Source **F** that Desmond Tutu was responsible for tougher economic sanctions against South Africa? Explain your answer carefully.

The United Democratic Front

What made the United Democratic Front so powerful?

Rebellion began in the classroom . . .

Black school children still had much to complain about: an age restriction on who could stay on at school, unqualified teachers and too many pupils in each class. Instead of being grateful to the government for putting more money into education to build more schools, black school children and college students united in 1979 to form the Congress of African Students (COSAS) and African university students formed the Azanian Students Organization. Between April 1980 and January 1981 one hundred thousand children in coloured and African schools and students from five black colleges boycotted classes. Community groups supported their protests.

Movement to the cities fuelled discontent

Pressure from employers led to relaxation of the pass laws. The removal of job reservations for whites and coloureds appeared to open up new job opportunities for Africans. The result was a sudden surge in the numbers of Africans leaving the homelands and settling in townships and in squatter camps closer to the big cities like Johannesburg and Cape Town. These newcomers increased competition for jobs and added to the expenses of local government, who had to house, educate and look after them. To make matters worse, by 1982 serious economic problems caused rising food prices, an increase in rents and high unemployment.

Source A Black townships and squatter camps in the Cape and Vaal triangle

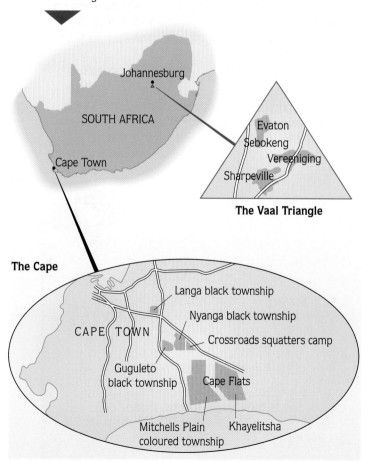

Source B The new constitution, 1984

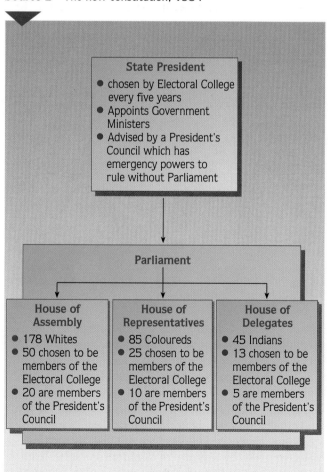

Black Community Councils and the new constitution

In 1982 the government gave Black Community Councils greater powers to raise rents and taxes. The very idea of continuing a system of local government which kept people of different races apart showed that Botha's government had no intention of scrapping apartheid. Blacks saw those who stood for election to the Community Councils as collaborators, and soon many councillors had a reputation for being corrupt. Meanwhile, the proposed new constitution (Source **B**) gave Indians and coloureds very little real power and excluded black people altogether.

Opposition to elections to the new community councils in 1983 and to the new Parliament in 1984 brought together young people, trade unionists and Churches into a movement called the United Democratic Front.

Representatives of over 500 organizations came together for the official launch of the movement in Mitchell's Plain outside Cape Town on 20 August 1983.

Source D   A UDF banner

Source C   The Reverend Allan Boesak, president of the World Alliance of Reformed Churches, at the launch on 20 August 1983

> Let me remind you of three little words . . . The first word is 'all'. We want *all* our rights . . . The second word is the word 'here'. We want all our rights *here* in a united, undivided South Africa. We do not want them in impoverished homelands . . . The third word is the word 'now'. We want all our rights, we want them here, and we want them now . . . We have been jailed, exiled, killed for too long. *Now* is the time.

The campaign against voting in elections to the Community Councils and new Parliament was a huge success. An average of only 21% of blacks voted in the elections for the twenty-four town councils in November 1983. Only 19% Indians and 29% of coloureds bothered to vote in elections to the new Parliament in August 1984. As a result most people did not think the Community Councils and the new Parliament had the right to claim any authority over them.

The Vaal uprising

The moderate leadership of the UDF, which included Albertina Sisulu (wife of Walter Sisulu) identified with the ideas of the Freedom Charter and the ANC.

However, the UDF soon found itself caught up in a major rebellion which began to turn violent. Conflict started in the townships of the Vaal triangle (Source **A**) in September 1984, but by 1985 had spread to the Orange Free State, the eastern Cape and then to Cape Town and Natal. Increases in rent and service charges by the Community Councils sparked off the conflict at a time of high unemployment and rising food prices. Angry mobs attacked black councillors, their homes and government buildings and the homes of the police. It seemed that an uprising had begun!

Questions

1   What is the link between each of the following which helps explain why a rebellion, started in the Vaal triangle in 1984, spread quickly to other parts of South Africa by 1985:
   - the creation of organizations to unite young blacks, township communities and workers;
   - relaxation of the pass laws;
   - the state of the economy;
   - Black Community Councils;
   - The new constitution;
   - The United Democratic Front (Sources **C** and **D**)?

2   What had changed to make the United Democratic Front a more serious threat to the government than the Freedom Charter Movement (see pages 36–9)?

Containing the violence

 Who was responsible for violence between blacks?

Key events during the last years of apartheid

1985 State of Emergency in parts of the country; Congress of South African Trade Unions (COSATU) formed

1986 1.5 million blacks stage largest strikes in South African history; Nationwide state of emergency; increased publicity given to vigilante violence and 'necklace killings'; censorship of media reports of political protest

1986–9 Widespread violence between Inkatha and UDF in Natal

The government declared states of emergency and sent in the the army to restore control. However, the violence which continued was not just directed against the government (Source **A**).

Vigilantes and gang violence

In townships and squatter camps like Crossroads (Source **B**) gangs of vigilantes formed to 'take control'. This led to violent clashes with rival gangs. Those who reported the grim cycle of killings became aware of the involvement of the South African police (Source **C**).

Source B Crossroads squatter camp

Source A Black deaths in political violence, 1984–8

Year	Total
1984	175
1985	879
1986	1298
Shot by police	412
Killed by other blacks	265
Burned bodies found	231
Other	390
1987	661
1988	1149
Shot by police	34
Killed by other blacks outside Natal	15
Burned bodies found	5
Killed in Natal conflict	912
Other	183

From the South African Institute of Race Relations, Annual Surveys

Source C Michael Buerk, BBC News, 25 January 1986

Most weekends I went to the funerals but none so menacing as the day they buried the radical chief Mayisa. The knives were out for his killers – a black gang which normally seemed to have police protection but not that day. I followed the mob as they chased one of the gang home. His family would not let him in but the mob wanted them too. They caught him. You can look away; I couldn't. A single blow rarely kills but death *is* sudden. One minute I was watching a terrified boy, the next a carcass. We knew that to interfere would mean death yet standing there witnessing them kill was perfectly safe. I knew the moment he died. I felt the spirit dissolve from his body. It wasn't just murder, it was revenge – the most depressing thing I have ever seen. More than violent death. The evil soul of man.

Rivalry between the ANC and Inkatha

The ANC saw Chief Buthelezi as a collaborator because he accepted a separate Zulu homeland for the Zulus, opposed economic sanctions against South Africa and opposed the ANC's use of violence. In 1980 the ANC split publicly with Inkatha. The exiled leader of the ANC made the following declaration in 1985.

Source D   Oliver Tambo on Radio Freedom, 1985

> We have to make apartheid ungovernable.

It became clear to Inkatha that the UDF was a close ally of the ANC.

Source E   Henry Khehla Mabhida, trade union organizer

> These people, armed with assegais and knobkerries [wooden sticks with a heavy wooden head], stopped in front of my house where I was standing . . . the leader of the group began swearing at me and hurling abuse at me. He told me that as my son was a member of the UDF he advised me to pack my belongings and to leave my house together with my family, failing which he and other members would return that night and evict my family and myself forcibly.
>
> **Quoted in *Inkatha: A Study*, IDAF, 1986**

Source F   Winnie Mandela shocked even many UDF supporters with her words in April 1986, speaking at the Kagiso township near Johannesburg

> The time for speeches and debate has come to an end. 1986 is going to see the liberation of the oppressed masses of this country. We work in the white man's kitchen. We bring up the white man's children. We could have killed them at any time we wanted to. Together, hand-in-hand with our sticks and our matches, with our necklaces, we shall liberate this country.

Source G   The victim of a necklace killing

The 'necklaces' to which she was referring were tyres filled with petrol which were rammed over a victim's shoulders and set alight (Source **G**).

Source H   Chief Buthelezi, letter to the *Guardian* [UK], 15 November 1986

> The ANC urges the assassination of black town councillors, policemen, members of the defence force and any other individual who disputes them. Part of its programme is to annihilate *Inkatha* and other black groups who oppose its tactics and strategies . . . they have been hacked to death, they have been necklaced, their houses have been burned to the ground . . . one can only expect violent reaction to violent onslaught.

Questions

1   How would the government have used Sources **A** to **H** to justify declaring a State of Emergency?

2   Which evidence helps to explain why the government survived in power?

3   Why did violent conflict develop between the ANC and Inkatha?

Why did P. W. Botha become a reformer?

▶ ## What did P. W. Botha hope his reforms would achieve?

P. W. Botha – key dates

1916	Pieter Willem Botha born in Orange Free State; parents farmers;
1948	elected MP for Nationalist Party
1958–66	held a number of junior minister posts
1966–78	Minister of Defence
1978–84	Prime Minister
1984	President with increased powers following creation of a new constitution.
1985	'Rubicon' speech.
1989	resigned as leader of the National Party, following a stroke, but remained President until after meeting with Mandela in August

Source A Rian Malan, an Afrikaner journalist who rebelled against the apartheid system which his family helped to create

▼

And then Pieter Willem Botha came to power. I wouldn't accuse Botha of loving blacks, but he was certainly more reasonable than any of his predecessors. One of Botha's first moves in office was to scrap the grand apartheid blueprint, which called for all blacks to be removed eventually from 'white' South Africa. He recognized blacks as permanent residents of white cities and granted them the right to own houses and property in the townships. He permitted the rise of a real black opposition and allowed hostile trade unions to organize openly . . . He rescinded [got rid of] some of the more odious apartheid laws and offered a vote of sorts to the coloured and Indians, hoping to make them allies in the struggle against blacks. He started pouring money into black education and easing restrictions on black enterprise, hoping to create a black middle class as a bulwark against revolution. To pay for all this he taxed white South Africans till it bled. In the first five years of his rule, black income rose five-fold, while white income barely kept pace with inflation. To whites who whined, PW had this to say: 'Adapt or die.'

From Rian Malan, *My Traitor's Heart*, 1990

Botha's reforms split the National Party. Dr Andries Treurnicht left the National Party to form the Conservative Party.

Source B Treurnicht's speech to the Congress of the Conservative Party, Bloemfontein, 15 August 1985

▼

You will be crushed between Black radical demands and White resistance which will refuse to be co-governed by non-Whites.

On the same day Botha made a famous speech in which he referred to 'crossing the Rubicon' – an expression from Roman history which means to decide on a course of action with irreversible consequences.

Source C   President P. W. Botha, Durban, National Party Natal Congress, 15 August 1985

▼

While the National Party respects the multicultural . . . nature of South Africa's population, it rejects any system . . . which amounts to one nation or group in our country dominating another or others . . . I stated in Parliament, when put this question, that if Mr Mandela gives a commitment that he will not make himself guilty of planning, instigating or committing acts of violence for the furtherance of political objectives, I will, in principle, be prepared to consider his release . . . My government and I are determined to press ahead with our reform programme . . . I believe that today we are crossing the Rubicon. *There can be no turning back.*

Botha regarded Communism as South Africa's most serious enemy.

Source D   P. W. Botha

▼

We hope to create a middle class among the nations of South Africa. Because, if a man has possessions and is able to build his family life around those possessions, then one has clearly laid the foundation for resisting communism. If anyone has something to protect, to keep as his own, then he fights communism more readily.

Quoted in an article by P. Hudson and Michael Sarakinsky in *South African Review* 3, Johannesburg: Ravan Press, 1986

In August 1989 Botha arranged a meeting with Nelson Mandela.

Source E   Nelson Mandela's record of the meeting with Botha

▼

I was tense about seeing Mr Botha. He was known as 'die Groot Krokodil' – 'the Great Crocodile' – and I had heard many accounts of his ferocious temper . . . The door then opened and I walked in expecting the worst . . .

From the opposite side of his grand office, P. W. Botha walked towards me. He had planned his march perfectly, for we met exactly halfway. He had his hand out and was smiling broadly, and in fact, from that first moment, he completely disarmed me. He was unfailingly courteous, deferential and friendly.

We very quickly posed for a photograph of the two of us shaking hands . . . Tea was served and we began to talk. . . We did not discuss substantive [big and important] issues so much as history and South African culture. I mentioned that I recently read an article in an Afrikaans magazine about the 1914 Afrikaner Rebellion, and mentioned how they had occupied towns in the Free State. I said I saw this struggle as a parallel to this famous rebellion, and we discussed this episode for quite a while. South African history, of course looks very different to the black man and white man. Their view was that the rebellion had been a quarrel between brothers, whereas my struggle was a revolutionary one. I said that it could also be seen as a struggle between brothers who happened to be different colours. The meeting was not even half an hour long . . . It was then I raised a serious issue. I asked Mr Botha to release unconditionally all political prisoners including myself. That was the only tense moment in the meeting, and Mr Botha said that he was afraid that he could not do that . . . Mr Botha rose and shook my hand, saying what a pleasure it had been. Indeed, it had been. I thanked him, and left the way I had come. While the meeting was not a breakthrough in terms of negotiations, it was one in another sense. Mr Botha had long talked about the need to cross the Rubicon, but he never did it himself until that morning . . . Now, I felt, there was no turning back.

From Nelson Mandela, *Long Walk to Freedom*, 1994

Questions

1 Use Source **A** to explain what Botha's reforms changed in South Africa.

2 To what extent does the evidence of this chapter support Andries Treurnicht's judgement in Source **B**?

3 Do you believe Botha intended to save or to eventually end apartheid (Sources **C** and **D**)? Explain your answer.

4 Study Source **E**.
a) Suggest why Nelson Mandela chose to discuss history and South African culture before the release of political prisoners?
b) Why do you think Nelson Mandela felt that there was no 'turning back' after his meeting with P. W. Botha?

11 The collapse of apartheid 1989–94

A new South Africa is born

▶ ## Why did de Klerk abolish apartheid?

'The time for talking . . .'

F. W. de Klerk (Source **A**) like Nelson Mandela, began his career as a lawyer.

In many ways de Klerk was an old-fashioned Afrikaner. When he replaced P. W. Botha as president in 1989, few thought he would make many changes.

F. W. de Klerk – key dates	
1936	born in Johannesburg; father a politician
1954	studied law
1958	travelled in Britain
1961–72	lawyer in Vereeniging
1969	married Marike Willemse; two sons
1972	elected MP
1984	Minister of Home Affairs
1989	elected leader of National Party; won election and became President
1993	awarded Nobel Peace Prize
1994	made Deputy President

Source A F. W. de Klerk becomes President, 20 September 1989

However, on 2 February 1990, de Klerk opened Parliament with a 35 minute speech which began to demolish the whole apartheid state. He unbanned the ANC, the PAC, the Communist Party and 30 other organizations; freed political prisoners and suspended the death sentence. Nine days later he released Nelson Mandela without conditions (Source **B**).

Source B Freedom at last, 11 February 1990

Source C President de Klerk's speech to Parliament, 2 February 1990

It is time for us to break out of the cycle of violence and break through to peace and reconciliation . . . a new democratic constitution; universal franchise; no domination; equality before the law . . . better education, health services, housing and social conditions for all. The time for talking has arrived.

'My God, he's done it all' I murmured to my colleague. My first thought was – and still is – that de Klerk didn't appreciate the full implications of what he was doing.

Allister Sparks, *Tomorrow is Another Country*, 1995

Over the next four years the apartheid state was dismantled. Some people called it a miracle.

Source E   Key developments in the collapse of apartheid

1990	May: racial segregation in health care ended
	June: Separate Amenities Act repealed
	July: Johannesburg City Council abolished housing segregation
	October: State of Emergency ended
1991	February: Group Areas Act and Land Act repealed
	June: Population Registration Act repealed
	March: referendum showed big majority for reform
	October: de Klerk apologized publicly for the 'sins of apartheid'
1993	January: government departments abolished all apartheid rules
	December: whites-only Parliament abolished
1994	April: multi-party, non-racial elections

Searching for causes

It is never easy to explain why a major change took place. Consider the following reasons:

A sudden conversion

At the religious service held to mark the beginning of his presidency, on 20 September 1989, de Klerk was in tears. Friends say he was seized by a 'calling from God' to save all the people of South Africa.

A clever strategy

Enormous problems faced de Klerk when he became president. Over 4000 people had been killed on the streets since 1985, 50,000 people were in prison without trial, troops were stationed in the townships, the economy was in deep trouble. De Klerk decided that ending apartheid would help to solve these problems and enable the white minority to hold on to power (see pages 86–7).

The message from the voters

In 1989 the National Party had the worst election result since 1948. For the future, they had to decide whether to support reform or return to strict apartheid to win back lost votes. De Klerk decided that reform would appeal to most voters.

Secret talks

By 1990 the government had held many secret meetings with Mandela and government advisers had met ANC leaders eleven times at a mansion called Mells Park near Bath in England.

President de Klerk's brother attended several meetings and reported to him. The two sides got on well and the government decided they could 'do business' with the ANC. The ANC felt the same.

The collapse of Russia

Government leaders said they could not trust the ANC because they were allies of Russia and wanted to spread Communism. In the late 1980s Gorbachev's reforms led to the break up of the Soviet Union.

Source F   De Klerk's speech to Parliament, 2 February 1990

Events in the Soviet Union and Eastern Europe weaken organizations which were previously supported strongly from those quarters.

However much people argued over the causes of de Klerk's decision there could be no doubt that the world had changed overnight.

Questions

1 Study Source **C**. Which words in the speech meant that de Klerk intended to abolish apartheid?

2 Using Sources **C** and **D** explain why the journalist thought that de Klerk did not appreciate the full effects of his speech.

3 Choose the three most important reasons why de Klerk abolished apartheid, and justify your choice.

From prisoner to President

▶ ## Why was white minority rule abandoned?

What were de Klerk's intentions?

President de Klerk often said that he had no intention of allowing power to pass to the black majority (Source **A**).

Source A De Klerk's speech at Transvaal Congress, *The Times*, 18 October 1990

▼

We reject black majority rule. We stand for power-sharing and group rights. We are not sellouts of anyone. We are going to make it safer for our descendants to live in South Africa.

How did de Klerk propose to share power? He said that everyone would vote for members of Parliament but the Senate, elected by the whites and tribal groups would have power to block any reforms they did not like. De Klerk and his advisers also secretly hoped that Mandela would rapidly lose popularity. They expected the ANC to break up. Thirdly, they planned to play off the two main African groups, the ANC and the Inkatha Freedom Party, against one another and emerge victorious (Source **B**).

Source B Mandela, de Klerk and Buthelezi, 14 September 1991

▼

Yet only four years after de Klerk's speech the country held its first multi-racial election and Mandela replaced de Klerk as President. Black majority rule was a reality.

Why did de Klerk give up white rule?

● It was impossible to stop the process of reform halfway. Black people had fought and died for freedom. Power-sharing was a fraud (Source **C**).

Source C Nelson Mandela, from *Long Walk to Freedom*, 1994

▼

I told de Klerk that . . . the ANC had not struggled against apartheid for seventy-five years only to yield to a disguised form of it . . . if it was his true intention to preserve apartheid through the Trojan horse of group rights, then he did not truly believe in ending apartheid.

● Mandela impressed people with his air of authority and his sensitivity. He was a born leader. Again and again he repeated the words of the Freedom Charter but he acknowledged the fears of white people (Source **D**).

Source D Nelson Mandela, in *The Times*, 12 February 1990

▼

Whites are fellow South Africans and we want them to feel safe and to know that we appreciate the contribution they have made towards the development of this country.

● The ANC negotiators showed extraordinary skill in overcoming problems. Negotiations lasted for almost two years (Source **E**).

Source E The negotiations – key dates

1990	May: first official meeting between government and ANC
1991	December: CODESA (Convention for a Democratic South Africa) began
1992	May: talks collapsed
	June: ANC organized 'mass action'
	September: de Klerk and Mandela met; officials met secretly
1993	March: talks began again
	November: new constitution agreed
1994	April: elections

There was deadlock on several occasions. For example, in May 1992, the government insisted on power-sharing, not majority rule. They would not change their minds. The ANC organized strikes, boycotts and stayaways. Cities came to a standstill. Then Joe Slovo proposed a brilliant compromise: power-sharing for five years, security of jobs for police, civil servants and the armed forces; strong local and regional councils. Negotiations began again. Within eight months the new constitution was agreed, virtually accepting majority rule.

Joe Slovo – key dates

1926	born in Lithuania, a Jewish family
1934	emigrated to South Africa to escape persecution
1942	joined the Communist Party
1947	qualified as a lawyer
1952	arrested and detained
1963–73	lived in London
1974	organized ANC guerilla fighters in Zambia
1980	labelled 'Public Enemy No 1' by government
1994	Minister of Housing
1995	died of cancer

● The government regarded Chief Buthelezi as an ally they could use against the ANC. In fact he was not reliable. He stayed away from CODESA meetings, his supporters were involved in numerous outbreaks of violence which the government was suspected of encouraging (see pages 90–1) and he tried to set up an alliance with the Conservative Party called COSAG (Concerned South Africans Group). He even talked of civil war. Public opinion was appalled. The government was discredited.

At last, on 27 April, the election was held. Buthelezi agreed to include the Inkatha Party at the last moment. Millions of South Africans stood patiently in long queues to vote (Source **F**). There were 19 parties.

Source F Waiting to vote

The ANC won 62.65% of votes, the National Party won 20.4% and Inkatha 10.5%. For five years these parties would form the government. A new country had been born.

Questions

1 Study Source **A**. Explain how de Klerk tried to prove he was not a 'sellout'.

2 Compare Sources **A** and **C**. How do they disagree about reform?

3 Compare the career of Joe Slovo with Nelson Mandela.

4 Explain how the ANC defeated the government's plan for power-sharing.

'A bloody conflict is inevitable' (General Viljoen)

▶ **How strong was the opposition?**

F. W. de Klerk faced fierce opposition.

Source A Dr Andries Treurnicht, leader of the Conservative Party, in *The Times*, 3 February 1990

It's insanity . . . we are going to mobilize every section of the white community to fight for our survival in freedom in our country . . . we have not got a boat waiting for us in the harbour to allow us to escape.

The Conservative Party believed in strict apartheid, separate homelands and no negotiations with ANC terrorists. Between November 1989 and February 1992 results from eight by-elections showed a large swing to the Conservatives. Treurnicht said de Klerk's reforms must be halted. De Klerk decided to test opinion in March 1992 (Source **B**).

Source B The referendum question, from *Staatskoerant*, 28 February 1992

ONDERSTEUN U VOORTSETTING VAN DIE HERVORMINGSPROSES WAT DIE STAATSPRESIDENT OP 2 FEBRUARIE 1990 BEGIN HET EN WAT GERIG IS OP 'N NUWE GRONDWET DEUR ONDERHANDELING?

DO YOU SUPPORT CONTINUATION OF THE REFORM PROCESS WHICH THE STATE PRESIDENT BEGAN ON 2 FEBRUARY 1990 AND WHICH IS AIMED AT A NEW CONSTITUTION THROUGH NEGOTIATION?

YES/JA

NEE/NO

The result showed huge support for the government. 85% of white electors voted and 68.6% of those supported reform. Thereafter the Conservative Party declined.

Paramilitary groups

As many as 200 white groups were formed to fight changes and use force if necessary. Some invented names to frighten the enemy – the Order of Death, the White Wolves, the White Liberators. The largest group, the Afrikaner Resistance Movement (the AWB – Afrikaner Weerstands Beweging), posed a serious threat to peace. It was started by Eugene Terre Blanche in 1973. They had their own symbol (Source **C**) and secret stores of weapons.

Source C
The AWB symbol. It has the same colours as the Nazi flag

Source D A journalist describes the menacing behaviour of the AWB at a meeting in Ventersdorp on 9 August 1991

A few minutes ago Terre Blanche strode on to a platform and started to denounce de Klerk. The crowd is ecstatic . . . Almost all of the men and a good many of the women have obeyed Terre Blanche's instruction and are carrying guns. Some are wearing pieces of sharpened metal strapped to their arms . . . Some are spitting at the police and shouting traitor.

Feargal Keane, *The Bondage of Fear*, 1994

By 1993 the AWB had 20,000 members. Terre Blanche was a spell-binding orator who had a hypnotic effect on his followers. However, he proved to be more like a comic than a great leader. He twice fell off his horse in front of TV cameras and in 1991 he announced the formation of the AWB air force with six single engine planes.

Murder

White extremists killed Chris Hani on 10 April 1993 (Source **E**). Hani was the popular and inspiring leader of the younger members of the ANC.

Source E The murder of Chris Hani, 10 April 1993

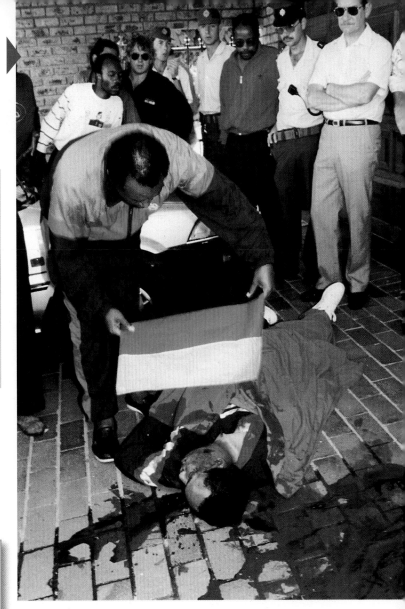

Chris Hani – key dates	
1942	born in the Transkei
1948–57	at school; wanted to be a priest
1957	joined ANC Youth League
1962	joined Umkhonto; arrested twice; escaped abroad
1967	trained guerilla fighters in Zambia
1987	Chief of Staff of Umkhonto
1990	returned home

An AWB member was charged with the murder because a white neighbour of the family phoned the police with the killer's number plate. That evening Mandela spoke to the nation on radio and television (Source **F**).

Source F Nelson Mandela, from *Long Walk to Freedom*, 1994

Now is the time for all South Africans to stand together against those who, from any quarter, wish to destroy what Chris Hani gave his life for – the freedom of all of us.

The battle of BOP

In March 1994, a month before the election, events in Bophuthatswana stunned the whole country. The ruler of this homeland had been a collaborator with the old apartheid regime and refused to join in the election. He appealed for help against his striking civil servants and police. AWB members rushed to the capital Mmabatho to answer his call. They wanted the opportunity to win a fight and to spoil the election. Within a day the local soldiers and police turned on the AWB, dragged them from their cars and shot them as they begged for mercy (Source **G**).

That night the whole nation saw on television the failure of the AWB to disrupt the peace process. The battle was a fiasco.

Source G AWB members face the end, 12 March 1994

Questions

1 Study Source **A**. What did Treurnicht mean by his last sentence?

2 Using Sources **E** and **F** explain how the murder of Chris Hani failed to destroy the peace process.

3 Compare Sources **D** and **G**. Describe how the public might react to each of these.

A painful birth

Why did violence continue?

Trouble in the townships

Between 1990 and 1994 more than 60,000 people died violently – more than were killed in the whole Boer war (Source **A**).

Source A The rising tide of violence

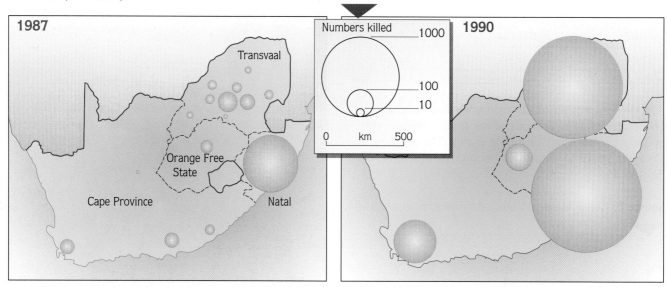

1987

Transvaal

Orange Free State

Cape Province

Natal

Numbers killed

1000
100
10

0   km   500

1990

Most incidents took place in the townships near Johannesburg and in Natal and many involved fights between ANC and IFP supporters. For example, in Phola Park, south of Johannesburg fourteen Inkatha members were massacred when they attended a rally at the football stadium, in September 1991. The IFP accused the ANC and blamed ex-Umkhonto fighters who had brought home their Russian AK 47 automatic rifles. For example, in Boipatong on 17 June 1992 armed Inkatha members crept out of the migrant workers' hostel and hacked, stabbed and shot 38 people to death in their homes. The victims included a nine-month-old baby, a child of four and 24 women (Source **B**).

Source B Burying the victims of the Boipatong massacre

Explanations

● The traditional rivalry between the Xhosa tribal group and the Zulus. Mandela, Tambo and Sisulu belonged to the Xhosa group; Buthelezi to the Zulus.
● A bitter feud between middle class town-dwelling ANC members and country-based old fashioned IFP members.
● A civil war secretly organized by the government to weaken the ANC, prove they were unfit to rule and make it necessary for the whites to continue in power.

Undoubtedly each of these played some part in the true explanation.

The ANC view

Mandela was certain that the government played a major role in encouraging the violence (Source **C**).

Source C Nelson Mandela, from *Long Walk to Freedom*, 1994

Of all the issues that hindered the peace process, none was more devastating and frustrating than the escalation of violence . . . The police were making very few arrests . . . Over and over again I heard the same story: the police were destabilizing an area. I was told of the police confiscating weapons one day in one area and the Inkatha forces attacking our people with those stolen weapons the next day. We had stories of the police escorting Inkatha members to meetings . . .

A government regulation, announced in 1991, added fuel to the flames. Zulus were allowed to carry their 'traditional weapons' to political rallies and meetings – assegais and knobkerries (wooden sticks with a heavy wooden head) (Source **D**).

The Inkatha view

At the same time Inkatha supporters were convinced the ANC was working with the government to frustrate the hopes of the 8.5 million Zulus for an independent home of their own (Source **E**).

Source E An IFP supporter

The ANC is behind the whole crisis. The war is between Xhosas and Zulus. The ANC only supports the Xhosas. If you are a Zulu they burn you . . . we are labelled AWB supporters. Meanwhile the ANC is in bed with the government. The ANC uses R1s and R5s security force guns. We don't know where they get them. The soldiers go around with two ANC members inside the Hippos (armed trucks)

Quoted in D. Reed, *Beloved Country*, 1994

The government view

President de Klerk said the police were totally fair. Their behaviour was above suspicion. Buthelezi said he could see nothing wrong with Inkatha members carrying the weapons Zulus always carried. Eventually, however, in October 1991, de Klerk appointed Judge

Source D Inkatha supporters ready for a fight

Richard Goldstone to investigate rumours of a 'Third Force' which was organising the violence on behalf of the government. Goldstone made several reports. He discovered a secret unit working to discredit ANC leaders. Twenty three senior army officers were suspended. He revealed the most dramatic evidence on 18 March 1994, a few weeks before the election (Source **F**).

Arms were given to Inkatha killers

South Africa suspends top police chiefs

Source F Headline in *The Times*, 19 March 1994

Goldstone accused senior police officers of organising a unit to distribute guns to the IFP and running a 'Third Force' aimed at sabotaging the country's progress to democracy. The judge was highly respected for his meticulous sifting of evidence. How much did de Klerk really know? Was this how he planned to abolish apartheid but still hold on to power?

Questions

1 What evidence does Mandela give to confirm his suspicions about the government helping Inkatha (Source **C**)?

2 What complaints does the IFP supporter have about the ANC (Source **E**)?

3 How did Goldstone's report confirm Mandela's suspicions (Source **C**)?

12 South Africa after apartheid

Facing the future

▶ **What problems remain?**

National unity

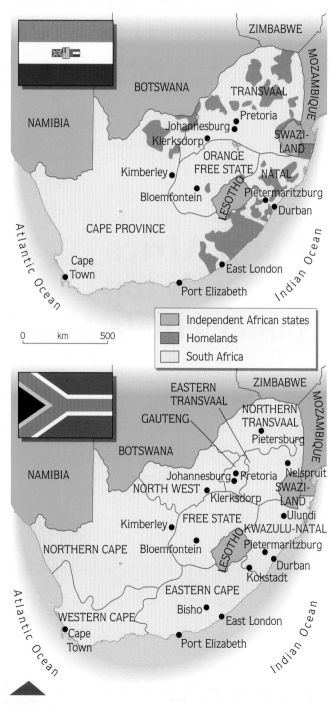

Source A   The old (top) and the new South Africa

Source B   Burying the past – a painting of Dr Verwoerd's cabinet being removed from Parliament in January 1996

The ANC won 62.6% of the votes in South Africa's first democratic General Election in 1994. However, Nelson Mandela not only wanted to bury the past (Source **B**) but to begin building a new South Africa in partnership with old enemies.

Source C   Nelson Mandela, from *Long Walk to Freedom*, 1994

I saw my mission as one of preaching reconciliation, of binding the wounds of the country . . . I knew that many people, particularly the minorities, whites, coloureds and Indians, would be feeling anxious about the future, and I wanted them to feel secure.

Nelson Mandela became President of South Africa on 10 May 1994. His government of National Unity included F. W. de Klerk, the leader of the white Afrikaner National Party, as one of two deputy presidents, and Chief Buthelezi, the Zulu leader of the Inkatha party, who became Minister for Home Affairs. Relations with these two politicians were not easy. In June 1996 F. W. de Klerk and the National Party left the government. Meanwhile, Buthelezi quarrelled with Mandela and violent feuding continued between the ANC and Inkatha in Natal.

Forgiveness and reconciliation?

Mandela made huge symbolic efforts to make whites feel valued and safe in South Africa after apartheid. Thousands of Afrikaner rugby fans cheered enthusiastically when he appeared in a Springbok jersey at the Rugby World Cup final in June 1995. He visited Betsie Verwoerd, the widow of the man who jailed him for life. Newspaper photographs showed her looking up at Mandela in admiration as she clasped his hand. However, there were signs during the visit that attitudes had not changed. The white elders of the town saw his visit as an act of recognition.

Source D   Mandela meets Mrs Verwoerd

Source E   The white elders presented Mandela with a petition

> . . . demanding that the whole of the Northern Cape be made a preferential settlement area for Afrikaners . . . the local primary schoolchildren were given the day off so that they could witness 'this historic visit by the head of state of a neighbouring country'.
>
> **From the *Guardian*, 22 August 1995**

A 'Commission of Truth and Reconciliation' chaired by Archbishop Desmond Tutu called upon victims of apartheid to forgive those guilty of crimes against them and their loved ones. This angered many people including the widow of Steve Biko (see page 67).

Source F   Ntsiki Biko, quoted in the *Independent on Sunday*, 31 March 1996

> What I want is for the proper course of justice to be done.

Poverty and inequality?

The new government introduced an ambitious programme of 'Reconstruction and Development'. It aimed to build new low-cost homes, to improve health and education and to redistribute 30% of the land within five years.

Sources **G** and **H** give two views of its progress in 1996.

Source G   Rushdie Magiet, development manager for the Western Province Cricket Association

> Apartheid is over and the government is changed but people's attitudes don't change overnight . . . The facilities in most townships are still terrible.
>
> **From the *Independent*, 30 January 1996**

Source H   George Warman, businessman January 1996

> Overseas investment is growing all the time. Tourism has more than trebled . . . The government has three priorities right now: Health, Education and Housing. And it is working hard on these: starter homes are being provided, funded by the government and building societies. They start as concrete shells which can be added to. Electricity is being provided . . . An important factor in the whole process is lack of bitterness and desire for revenge . . . Mandela provides an excellent role model of forgiveness in his efforts to 'nation-build'.

Questions

1   What do Sources **A**, **B**, **C**, **D** and **H** show had changed in South Africa since the fall of apartheid?

2   Explain the anger of Ntsiki Biko (Source **F**).

A rimbow nation

▶ **Can integration defeat racism?**

Source A Integrated: South African school-children

Desmond Tutu used the phrase 'rainbow people' to describe his ideal of a racially mixed South Africa.

By 1995 the defeat of apartheid had not got rid of racial segregation in South Africa. Ventersdorp is a two hours drive north west of Johannesburg.

Source B A journalist reports his visit to a Ventersdorp hotel in December 1995

▼

I ask the bar-tender . . . about the bar down the road, and he stares at me like a wolfhound that has just heard a funny noise. 'It's a shebeen,' he says after a while. 'It's for non-whites. You drink here.' There is a finality in his voice and a look in his eye which say, 'No more stupid questions.'

Robert Block, *Independent on Sunday*, **28 January 1996**

Source C Also in Ventersdorp, a white woman spoke to the reporter

▼

I don't mind if they have manners. If they have manners they are welcome in my home. The old ones I can talk to because they say, 'Marie, I know I'm a kaffir. But say kaffir to the young ones and they'll take you to court.'

Robert Block, *Independent on Sunday*, **28 January 1996**

In February 1996 at Potgietersrus Primary school (Source **A**) white parents lost a court battle to prevent 16 black children joining the school.

After Mandela?

Source D The British Prime Minister, Margaret Thatcher, in 1987

The ANC is a typical terrorist organization . . . Anyone who thinks it is going to run the government in South Africa is living in cloud-cuckoo land.

Conservative politicians who shared this view also saw Mandela as a terrorist.

Source E A British Conservative MP

Nelson Mandela should be shot.

Quoted in the *Independent*, 9 July 1996

However, in 1996 there were fears about the future of South Africa without Nelson Mandela.

Source F From the *Independent*, 6 March 1996

SA holds its breath for Mandela medical

South Africans and investors of all colours across the globe crossed their fingers yesterday as President Mandela began three days of tests aimed at quashing rumours that his health is failing.

When Nelson Mandela made a state visit to Britain in July 1996 (Source **G**) enthusiastic crowds turned out to greet him. Politicians of all parties, including Margaret Thatcher, came to listen to him speak to the two Houses of Parliament. Part of the reason for his visit was to encourage British businesses to invest in South Africa. Some 400 businessmen gathered to meet him.

Source G Nelson Mandela meets admirers during his state visit to Britain in 1996

Source H From the *Independent*, 11 July 1996

By the time he had finished his address the audience were on their fourth standing ovation, . . . among their ranks were some, perhaps many, who had helped prop up the apartheid regime for nearly half a century and had thus helped to keep their hero incarcerated on Robben Island.

It is difficult to imagine whether anyone other than Nelson Mandela could have brought off the peaceful transition from white minority rule to black rule. Rarely in history has there been a politician who has held such worldwide respect. What does the future hold for South Africa after Mandela?

Questions

1 What do Sources **E**, **F** and **G** (page 93), and **B** and **C** show had not changed in the new South Africa?

2 How do you explain fears for the future of South Africa 'after Mandela' (Source **F**)?

3 a) In what way does Source **H** suggest that the attitudes of many British businessmen towards Mandela have changed?
   b) How do you explain these attitudes?

4 What problems does South Africa face without Nelson Mandela?

Index

African nationalism 20–3, 24
Afrikaans 8, 13, 19, 26, 68
Afrikaner nationalism 19, 24–7, 30–3
ANC 22, 24–5, 36–9, 42, 48–9, 54–7, 61–2,
 66, 70, 76, 80, 84, 86–7, 90–4
ANC Youth League 24–5, 36, 59, 69
Angola 61, 66, 75–6
Anti-apartheid movement 41
Anti-pass campaign 50, 54
apartheid, meaning 4, 32, 43–5
Atlantic Charter 59
AWB 88–9

Bambatha rebellion 20
banning orders 38, 42, 49, 53, 66
Bantu Self Government Act 42
Bantustans 42, 45–6, 52, 65, 69, 72
Biko, Steve 66–7
Black Consciousness 66–8
Black Sash 48
Blood River 14, 28, 30
Boer War 17–9, 56
Boesak, Allan 79
BOSS 56, 72, 76
Botha, P.W. 74–5, 82–3
Broederbond 26, 28
bus boycott 51
Buthelezi, Gatsha 69, 87, 91–2

censorship 42, 65
Cold War 62
Coloureds 8, 12–3, 20, 36, 38, 44, 51, 75
Communism 32, 34, 54, 62, 66, 76–7
Conservative Party 74, 82, 87–8
Constitution, new 75, 78–9
COSAS 75, 78
COSATU 80

de Klerk 6, 84–5, 86–7, 88–9, 92
defiance campaign 36–7
Dutch East India Company 9, 12–3

Education 34–5, 75, 78, 94
Emergency, State of 48, 55, 80, 85

Freedom Charter 38–9, 49
Freedom Day 36

Gandhi, M.K. 20–1, 36
Goldstone Enquiry 91
Great Trek 14, 24, 30–1
Group Areas Act 34, 51, 85
guerilla warfare 66, 76
Gwangqua, Battle of 14–5

Hani, Chris 89
Hertzog, General 24–6
Homelands 65, 72
Huddleston, Trevor 40–1

Immorality Act 34
Indians 9, 14–5, 20–1, 36, 38, 51, 54, 75, 82

Inkatha 69, 86–7, 90–1

Johannesburg 10, 21, 26, 28, 36, 38, 54,
 68, 78
Joseph, Helen 50, 53

Khoikhoi 9, 13
Kruger, President 31
KwaZulu 69

Land Act 1913 22, 85
Lembede, Anton 24, 59
Lutili, Albert 38, 49, 51, 54–6, 58, 62

Macmillan, Harold 46, 61
Malan, Dr 24–6, 28, 31–3
Malan, Magnus 75
Mandela, Nelson 5–6, 36, 49, 56–7, 70–1,
 75, 83–5, 87, 92–4
Mandela, Winnie 56, 71, 81
Mfecane 9
Milner, Lord 19–20, 58
minerals 62, 76
Mines and Works Act 21
Mixed Marriages Act 1949 34
MK 48, 56
Mozambique 61, 66, 76
Muldergate scandal 72–3

Namibia 76–7
Natal 9, 14, 20
National Day of Protest 36
Native Law Amendment Act 34
Native National Convention (ANC) 22
Native Resettlement Act 51
Native Urban Areas Act 25
Necklaces 81
Ngoyi, Lilian 50
Nguni 9
Nkomati Accord 76
Nkosi Sikelel' 22
nuclear power 76–7

oil 63–4
Olympic Games 61
Orange Free State 9, 14, 16
Organisation of African Unity (OAU) 61
Ossewa Brandweg 25, 72

PAC 42, 48, 54, 66, 69, 70
pass burning 21, 24
Pass Laws 21, 34–5, 44–5, 48, 50–1, 74, 78
peasant revolts 48, 52
police 37–8, 40, 42, 67–8, 72–3
poor whites 28–9, 64
Population Registration Act 34, 85
Poqo 56
Purified National Party 26, 28

racism 58–9
removals 45
Representation of Natives Act 1936 24

republic 47
reserves 22–3, 52
Rhodes, Cecil 16
Rhodesia 61, 66, 76
Rivonia Farmhouse and Trial 56–7, 70
Robben Island 9, 66, 70–1

San 9, 13
Sanctions 61–2, 77
SASO 67
schools 35, 68, 75, 78
segregation 28, 32
Separate Amenities Act 34, 85
Sharpeville 48, 54–7
Sisulu, Albertina 79
Sisulu Walter 36, 56–7, 70–1
Slovo, Joe 49, 56, 66, 87
Smuts, General 21, 24, 32, 59
Sobukwe, Robert 54, 69
Sophiatown 40–1, 51
Soweto 10, 43, 68, 72
South West Africa 61, 76
Soviet Union 62–3, 76–7, 85
Strijdom, J. 50
Suppression of Communism Act 34
Suzman, Helen 71
SWAPO 61, 76

Tambo, Oliver 36, 66, 81
Terre Blanche, Eugene 88
Thatcher, Margaret 77
'Third Force' 91
'Total Strategy' 74–5
Torch Commando 36
trade unions 64, 72, 74, 80, 82
Transvaal 9, 14, 16, 21, 51–2
Treason Trial 48–9
Treurnicht, Andries 74, 82, 88
Tutu, Desmond 40, 76–7, 93

Umkhonto we Sizwe 48, 56, 89
union 21
United Democratic Front 78–9, 81
United Nations 59, 61, 66, 76
United Party 24, 32

van Riebeeck 12, 36
Verwoerd, Hendrick 35, 42, 46–8, 52, 55,
 59, 61, 71, 92–3
Voortrekker monument 31
Vorster, B.J. 59, 72–3
voting system 20–1

Wiehahn Commission 72

Xhosa 9, 14, 90–1

Youth League 24–5, 59, 69

Zulus 9, 14, 17, 30, 90–1
Zimbabwe 76